ALTERNATIVES TO VIOLENCE

ALTERNATIVES TO VIOLENCE

A Stimulus to Dialogue

TIME-LIFE BOOKS, NEW YORK

Published simultaneously in Canada.
Library of Congress catalogue card number 68-57111.

PREFACE

The purpose of this book is to stimulate dialogue. It does not attempt to present a comprehensive study in depth but rather to provide an overview to serve as a catalyst for further creative thinking and effective action. Approximately 80 invitations were issued by the Committee for Alternatives to Violence to individuals in many fields and disciplines. They responded with essays specifically written for this book or, in some cases, excerpts from previously published material that the authors considered particularly relevant to contemporary problems. Those who could not accept were governed by heavy prior commitments or time limitations. None declined because of disinterest. Lack of representation of any particular point of view therefore is definitely unintentional. Likewise, the viewpoints presented are those of the individual contributors, and are not the responsibility of the other contributors, the editor, the Committee or the publisher.

Above all, this book is a tribute to our contributors. It is tangible evidence of their involvement and cooperation. Despite extraordinary pressures, a deadline that was anything but reasonable was met. The completion of this book in a four-month period testifies to a spirit of vital concern with the climate of violence that pervades the world.

Our profound gratitude goes to friends and colleagues who gave their help, advice and encouragement; to Barry Bryant, Virginia Dwan, John W. Mudd, Paula and Kent G. Smith, Linda and Ward Stanley and Wendy Watriss, who participated in the early discussions on this project; and in particular to Gordon D. Sharp Jr., of Princeton, New Jersey, who advised on the project throughout its duration. It is our sincere hope that they and others interested will continue with us in the work of the World Man Fund that has eventuated as a result of this entire endeavor.

COMMITTEE FOR ALTERNATIVES TO VIOLENCE

Larry Ng, M.D., Editor
Department of Neurology
Hospital of the University of Pennsylvania
3400 Spruce Street
Philadelphia, Pennsylvania 19104

Francois Bucher, Ph.D.
Associate Professor of Art and Archeology
Princeton University, N.J.

Harold D. Lasswell, Ph.D., Litt.D., L.L.D.
Ford Foundation Professor of Law and the
Social Sciences
Yale University, New Haven

Emily H. Mudd, M.S.W., Ph.D., Sc.D.
Professor of Family Study in Psychiatry
School of Medicine
University of Pennsylvania

B. Perry Ottenberg, M.D.
Chairman Social Issues Committee
Group for the Advancement of Psychiatry

ADAM THE INVENTOR by Pete Seeger

Irregular, traditional ballad style.

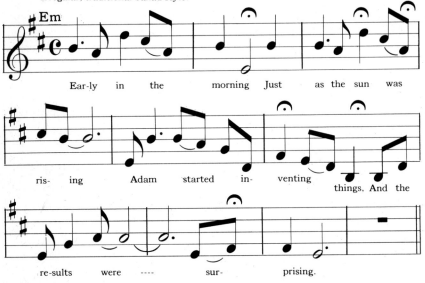

Ear-ly in the morning Just as the sun was ris- ing Adam started in- venting things, And the re-sults were ---- sur- prising.

1.
Early in the morning
Just as the sun was rising
Adam started inventing things
And the results were surprising.

2.
Later in the morning
The sun was getting higher
Adam made a discovery
He learned to handle fire.

3.
Invented spears, invented guns
Invented arrow and bow
And what it is now he's going to invent
I'm not sure I want to know.

4.
Invented language, invented words
Invented alphabets
But when it comes to communicating
Sometimes he was deaf.

5.
Conquered desert, conquered ice
Conquered ocean and shore
Conquered every animal beside himself
Then Adam invented war.

6.
Adam, brilliant Adam
So brilliant, you're made blind
Inventing some new kind of world
With no place for mankind.

7.
Stamp your foot, we've got one earth
One big red apple to share
All around us one ocean of water
And just one ocean of air.

8.
Can we break the grip of the Dance of
    Death?
Can this world be released?
Will Adam's children, the young
    inventors,
Will they now invent peace?

9.
Now some will scoff and some will scorn
But what makes them so certain?
Adam's children might surprise us all
And build anew the Garden.

Words: PETE SEEGER, SANTIAGO
GENOVÉS, WOLF RILLA
Tune adapted from British Traditional
© 1968 by Stormking Music, Inc.

You are violent.

I am violent.

We are all violent.

This book is about *our* violence.

The problem of violence is for real.

It is here, now and everywhere.

It is in us, from us, and by us.

It is alive as long as we are.

Concern is the reason for this book.

You are concerned, or you would not be reading this book.

Larry Ng, M.D.
Editor

CONTENTS

ALTERNATIVES

THE BASIS OF VIOLENCE

ON THE SOURCES OF HUMAN DESTRUCTIVENESS

Adapted from an unpublished manuscript.

by Erich Fromm

Erich Fromm is a psychoanalyst and author of *The Sane
Society* and *May Man Prevail? An Inquiry into the
Facts and Fictions of Foreign Policy.*

The assumption that human destructiveness is rooted in a destructive
instinct is untenable regardless of whether it is presented in terms of
Freud, Konrad Lorenz or modern classic psychoanalysts who think in
terms of a "destructive instinct" rather than in those of the "death instinct." Aside from neurophysiological factors that speak against this
hypothesis, the psychological and anthropological data seem to speak
against it. Freud's theory of the death instinct versus Eros, with
which all living beings—and not only man—are endowed, is very ques-
tionable if we consider the data of animal psychology. Following this
hypothesis we would have to assume that those animals which show
less aggression toward the outside discharge their aggression inside.
That would mean the less aggressive an animal is against others, the
more it would suffer from illness or early death or any other sign of aggression towards itself. There is nothing to support this idea.

As far as the hypothesis of Lorenz is concerned, and the same holds
true for psychoanalysts who assume that there is a destructive instinct
charged with a spontaneously increasing energy demanding discharge,
the facts most in contrast to this assumption are the tremendous vari-
ability in aggressiveness among individuals and various societies. All
clinical individual and social evidence shows there are individuals and
societies that are characterized by a great deal of aggressiveness, either toward the outside or against themselves, and others that are
characterized by a relative lack of destructiveness and aggressiveness—
again in both directions. If there were an instinctual source analogous
to hunger and sex, these differences could hardly be explained.

As far as the evolutionary aspect of aggressiveness and destructiveness
is concerned, the analogies of Lorenz—brilliant as they often are—do

not adequately explain why man is so much more destructive and aggressive than any animal species. In fact, if the destructiveness of man were on a level with that of the primates, there would be little reason to worry about the fate of mankind.

As a result of these considerations, I arrive at the conclusion that the specific human aggressiveness—both quantitatively and qualitatively—is primarily due to the specific conditions of human existence, i.e., to the particular functioning of the system "Man." (In saying this I do not mean, of course, to deny that aggressiveness and destructiveness have their neurophysiological and chemical basis in the human organism like all other affects, but this only means that the *possibility* for destructive behavior is given in the human organism, not its *necessity*.)

The discussion about destructiveness and aggressiveness suffers in general from the lack of discrimination between various kinds of destructiveness. Such a discrimination is possible only from a dynamic viewpoint, and it is very difficult from a merely behavioristic viewpoint. The quality of various types of destructiveness is related to the causes for it. And in order to understand these different causes, one has to have a picture of the whole system Man as one of structured energy, a system that we usually call character if the concept of character is used in a dynamic sense. Clinical observation of various types of destructiveness in relation to the specific causes that act as stimuli can help in recognizing that the phenomena that usually are subsumed under the category of aggression, aggressiveness and destructiveness are among themselves qualitatively entirely different, even if they are sometimes overlapping.

In the following I mention some of the categories of aggressiveness and destructiveness that I find on the basis of clinical observation.

It should be noted that there are aggressive acts without aggressive motivation in a psychological sense. Examples are the duel, certain types of war games among primitives, Zen Buddhist sword fighting, etc.

Reactive aggression, i.e., aggression in response to threats to vital interests, is basically the same as that found in the animal. It has developed phylogenetically and serves the interest of life, both of the species and of the individual. There is, however, an important difference between animal and human reaction. The animal reacts with aggressiveness (unless it reacts with fear and flight) when its life, territory, access to females or its young are threatened. These threats must constitute a "clear and present danger" to stimulate the fight reaction. Man reacts semi-instinctively in the same way to all threats to his vital interests. The difference, however, lies in the following directions.

Being endowed with awareness of the future and imagination, man feels threatened not only by "clear and present dangers" but also by dangers that he visualizes as arising in the future. (If such visualization is based exclusively on logic and not on the principle of empirical likelihood, we deal with paranoid thinking.)

Man, building a civilization that is much more complex than that of the animal, also feels threatened in his vital interests when his property, his political freedom, etc. are the object of the threat.

Closely related is the third element characteristic of man. Inasmuch as he is a "symbol-making animal," symbols become as important to him as life, territory, and so on. Whether it is God, his country, his mother, his philosophical ideas or his picture of himself, he feels threatened insofar as these symbols or values have become vitally important to his mental equilibrium, that is, in defense of his sanity.

Eventually, due to his suggestibility, which is based on the use of symbols, man can be induced by his leaders to believe that he is threatened in his vital interests—though, in reality, he may not be.

All these facts that show that the experience of a threat to vital interests is in man much more frequent than in the animal tend to explain to some extent the greater amount of aggressiveness in man as compared with animals—although the basic mechanism of response to threats is the same.

Speaking about the quality of this reactive hostility, it can be said to be essentially self-limiting. It is a reaction to a threat from the outside, and it tends to disappear when the threat either ends by itself or has been removed by aggressive action.

Entirely different from reactive hostility are those forms of aggressiveness-destructiveness that are not reactions to outside threats but to certain forms of systemic dysfunction in man.

The most important among those is the kind of destructiveness that results from a sense of impotence, worthlessness, lack of enjoyment in life. One form of this type of destructiveness is *sadism*. Sadism is considered in this context not in the Freudian sense of a pregenital, partial sexual drive, but as an impulse—the aim of which is control over another human being or, for that matter, any living being or even things. This control can even be benevolent; more often it tends to strangle, choke, tie up the other person. To inflict pain is only one particular form of control. There is no greater power over another person than to make him suffer without his being able to defend himself. The wish for absolute control may lead to the wish to destroy the other person or things. Sadism in this broad sense is an expression of a desire for omnipotence, which is to be found in people who have a deep sense of impotence and who, in fact, are greatly limited by circumstances inside or outside of themselves in any productive act or relationship. Their only way of overcoming an unbearable sense of impotence (often related to conscious or unconscious depression) is the satisfaction of the wish for omnipotence (in which all limitations are removed by the fact that they can control, manipulate or destroy those who are weaker at the moment).

The sadistic action carries with it a high degree of satisfaction. For the person who in all his life feels impotent and incapable of affecting anything outside himself, the one moment of omnipotence often is worth risking or losing his life. On the other hand, certain social situations give individuals the sense of omnipotence, not just for a moment but sometimes for many years, provided they acquire absolute power over the rest of their group. An excellent example of this kind of sadistic omnipotence has been shown by Camus in the title character of his *Caligula,* who has absolute power; but because he has absolute power, he wants to transcend the limitations of human existence—"he wants the moon." His final insanity is not so much a sickness as a way of life induced by the possibility of unlimited power. Examples of omnipotent sadism are only too frequent in the history of man. They are found in acts of individuals against those who are weaker, especially children, animals and, in patriarchal societies, women; of racial majorities against minorities; of conquerors against the conquered.

Closely related to omnipotent sadism is *ecstatic hate*. For many individuals and cultures, the state of ecstasy is the principal answer to the problem of human existence. In the state of ecstasy the individual overcomes the split between himself and the world around him since his awareness and consciousness do not make him hesitant and doubtful. He becomes one, all his energies channeled in one direction. The state of ecstasy can be produced by drugs, rhythm, sex or auto-suggestion. It can also be produced by such a complete dedication to one goal that everything else is forgotten. All these forms of ecstacies are essentially benevolent because they are expressions of life, and often they enhance the intensity of the life experience.

There is only one truly malevolent form of ecstasy and that is the ecstasy of hate. The person who gives himself completely to hate, destruction and revenge is "beside himself" and thoroughly unified by the absoluteness of his hate. However, giving himself to hate and destruction, he loses contact with the world outside him and also with his own self. In many phenomena of destructiveness this ecstatic quality can be observed (e.g., the wave of blood-thirsty mass killing of Communists—alleged or real—and Chinese in Indonesia a few years ago).

What is characteristic of the omnipotent and ecstatic hate is that it is rooted in pathological elements in man's character structure, that it is not caused by stimuli from the outside but rather seizes upon them when the satisfaction of the sadistic impulse is possible; that the act itself has a high degree of visceral excitement and satisfaction that is not to be found in reactive aggressiveness. It seems that this type of destructiveness is specifically human because its premises—the sense of impotence, hopelessness, boredom, etc.—are typical of the system Man but not of the system "Animal." It follows that all efforts to change destructiveness of the sadistic-ecstatic type must be based on change within the character structure—which usually necessitates changes within the social structure. If individuals or social classes are left hope-less and powerless, one must expect them to react with destructiveness until conditions are changed. If life is too boring, the ecstacies of hate might become the preferred response. Omnipotent sadism and ecstatic hate cannot be cured by punishment but only by making life more in-teresting and by restoring to individuals the sense of potency.

While the forms of aggressiveness which I have described thus far are still attempts to assert life, even though sometimes in a perverse manner, there is another kind of destructiveness, which is not striving towards life but towards death. There are people who are attracted to death, decay, illness, to all that is not life, who in fact hate life in all its manifestations. These "necrophilous" people love death or the non-alive in contrast to the "biophilous" people who love life in all its manifestations, in its tendency for unification and structuring. Clinically the more extreme forms of necrophilia can easily be detected in dreams or the Rorschach test. In a milder form the necrophilous orientation can be seen in a strong attachment to all that is mechanical and to gad-gets, as against persons and all that is alive.

From my observation it seems that there is in many people a con-flict between necrophilous and biophilous tendencies, which is often resolved in favor of the biophilous side. In some individuals, however, it seems that the necrophilous side is so strong and unchangeable that I suspect constitutional factors play a considerable role. A great deal of further research needs to be done to study the causes of necrophilia. As to its difference from the sadistic-ecstatic destructiveness, it is to be noted that the necrophilic destructiveness lacks the excitement and the passionate character of the sadistic-ecstatic destructiveness. One might say that it is rather cold and dry as compared with the pas-sionate heat of the other type of destructiveness.

One concluding remark: while I have tried to describe schematically and briefly some main types of aggressiveness and destructiveness, I did not mean to imply that they are mutually exclusive. On the con-trary, they are sometimes blended. It is of particular importance to notice that some of the deeper and more irrational forms of aggressiveness can be triggered by more superficial and less irrational forms. Reactive hostility can and often does trigger sadistic-ecstatic hostility. Many people would be prevented from giving expression to their sadistic desires if it were not for the first step, which permits them to violate the normal taboo on violence and killing. Every war shows this phenomenon, but it also shows that probably in the majority of people the first step of aggressiveness does not trigger sadistic-ecstatic forms of destructiveness. Only extended studies could show the incidence of the sadistic-ecstatic and the necrophilous potential in a normal population and/or various sub-groups within it.

THE PREDICAMENT OF MAN

Given as the Sonning Award Address to the University of Copenhagen.
by Arthur Koestler

Arthur Koestler is the author of *Darkness at Noon, Insight and Outlook: an Inquiry into the Common Foundations of Science, Art, and Social Ethics, The Act of Creation* and *The Ghost in the Machine.*

In a recent book I advanced the unpopular hypothesis that the native equipment of *Homo sapiens* may contain some built-in error or deficiency that would predispose him to self-destruction. More precisely, that evolution has equipped our species with a type of brain in which affect-based beliefs are dissociated from and in perpetual conflict with the reasoning intellect. The result, as we see it, is a split-minded or schizophrenic mentality, which seems to be inherent in man's condition and is reflected in his absurd and tortured history. If this diagnosis is correct—and I think there is sufficient evidence from both history and neurophysiology to support it—then we would at least have a realistic base line to start the search for a cure.

We know that among social animals fighting is a ritualized affair that stops short of serious injury. The prey that the predator kills always belongs to a different species. Murder *within* the species on an individual or collective scale is a phenomenon unknown in the whole animal kingdom, except for man and a few varieties of ants and rats.

Evidently something must have gone wrong at some point in the evolution of *Homo sapiens*. But when we ask what it is that has gone wrong, we usually get the dusty answer that all evil stems from the selfish, greedy, aggressive tendencies in human nature. That is the explanation that has been offered to us for the last three thousand years by Hebrew prophets, Indian sages, Christian moralists and contemporary psychoanalysts; but speaking in all humility, I find this answer unconvincing and unsupported by the historical record. What the record indicates is that in the major disasters in our history, individual aggressiveness for selfish motives played an almost negligible part compared to unselfish loyalty and devotion to tribe, nation, religion or political ideology. Tribal wars, national wars, civil wars, religious wars, world wars, are waged in the purported interest of the community, not of the individual, to decide issues that are far removed from the personal self-interest of the combatants. No doubt the lust for rape and plunder provided occasional incentives for a minority, but for the great majority the primary motive was fanatical loyalty, to the point of self-sacrifice, to king and country, leader or group. In other words, the main trouble with man appears to be not that he is an excessively aggressive creature, but an excessively loyal one. He seems to have stronger biological needs than any other species to belong, to attach himself to a person, a group or idea, to transcend the claustrophobic confines of self. He cannot live alone, and he cannot leave alone.

One possible reason for this tendency may be the protracted helplessness and dependence of the human infant. Another reason may be the increased dependence on solidarity and cooperation of our primate ancestors when they turned into carnivorous hunters of prey bigger and faster than themselves. Primate societies living in the wild are also held together by strong bonds, and groups of the same primate species living in different localities may also develop different traditions and customs. But the cohesive bonds within primate families do not grow into neurotic attachments, the cohesive forces within primate groups do not attain the intensity and fervor of tribal feeling, and the differences between primate groups of the same species do not lead to violent conflicts. Only in *Homo sapiens* did the cohesive forces within the group develop into fanatical loyalty to tribe, totem and its later symbolic equivalents; and only in our species did the repellent forces between groups develop into intra-specific warfare.

What I am trying to suggest is that the aggressive, self-assertive tendencies in the emotional life of the human individual are less dangerous to the species than his self-transcending or integrative tendencies. Most civilizations throughout our history have been quite successful in taming individual aggressiveness and teaching the young how to sublimate their self-assertive impulses. But we have tragically failed to achieve a similar sublimation and canalization of the self-transcending emotions. The number of victims of individual crimes committed in any period of history is insignificant compared to the masses cheerfully sacrificed *ad majorem gloriam,* in blind devotion to the true religion, dynasty or political system. When we speak of "blind devotion" we implicitly recognize the uncritical nature of the self-transcending urge in forming attachments to a person, group, race, flag or system of beliefs. Every man is an island, craving to become attached to the mainland— or an atom with a free valency in search of a chemical bond. A privileged minority may achieve self-transcendence through the "oceanic feeling," the cathartic experiences mediated by the pursuit of science and art. But history shows that for the vast majority of mankind the only outlet for the self-transcending urge, the longing to belong, is a primitive form of identification with a social group and with the system of beliefs that it represents. There is an essential difference between such primitive identification and the mature forms of social integration. Integration preserves the autonomy and responsibility of the individual in the social whole; identification implies a partial or total sacrifice of both, a surrender of the critical faculties and of moral responsibility.

In some respects it represents a regression to infancy or even the "womb" of the church, as the saying goes; in other respects it resembles the hypnotic rapport; in extreme cases it produces the phenomena of mass hysteria in overt or latent form. One need not be physically present in a crowd to be affected by crowd mentality; it permeates the climate, like radioactive fallout, even in the privacy of one's bathroom.

Thus during most of human history, the self-transcending urges of the individual could only express themselves through devotion to a narrowly defined group, with which he identified himself to the hostile exclusion of other groups; as a result, the disruptive forces have always dominated the forces of cohesion in our species as a whole. The main peril of self-transcending devotion is that it frequently acts as a vehicle for a vicarious, unselfish kind of aggression. We enter into an identificatory rapport with the hero on the movie screen, and as a result hate the perfidious villain; our anger is a vicarious emotion experienced on behalf of another person who does not even really exist, and yet we produce all the physical symptoms of a true emotion. Similarly, the emotion displayed by a crowd of demonstrators is an unselfish type of emotion derived from the identification of the individual with the group. When alone, man is inclined to act in his own interest; when identified with a group, the situation is reversed. The egotism of the group feeds on the altruism of its members.

Human history is pockmarked with the scars of this infernal dialectic. As to its origins, some clues are perhaps provided by the biological factors previously mentioned: the long infantile dependence and strong social interdependence characteristic of our species; and the peculiarity of the human brain to sustain affect-based belief-systems that are incompatible with its reasoning faculties but nevertheless coexist with them. Let me mention briefly two further factors that seem to be equally basic to the human predicament.

The first is the emergence of language as an exclusively human blessing and curse. Language promotes communication and understanding within the group; but it also accentuates the differences in tradition and beliefs between groups and erects separative barriers between tribes, nations, regions, social classes. The Tower of Babel is an archetypal symbol of the process that turns the blessing into a curse and prevents man from reaching into heaven. According to Margaret Mead, among the two million Aborigines in New Guinea, 750 different languages are spoken in 750 villages that are at permanent war with one another. Even more dangerous, however, than the divisive effect of different vocabularies is the power of language to crystallize the implicit habits and ways of life of different communities into explicit doctrines and moral imperatives. If the citizens of Lilliput had not been blessed with language, they could not have fought a war over which end to break the egg because they would not have been able to transform a habit into an ideology.

Equal in importance to the discovery of language and of the use of tools is man's discovery of death. But we should rather say: the discovery of death by the intellect and its rejection by instinct. Instinct takes existence for granted and cannot conceive of nonexistence. The affect-charged refusal to accept death as a natural and final phenomenon became a dominant motive in all human cultures, and a paradigm of the split mind. It populated the atmosphere with invisible presences, most of them malevolent or at least capricious and unpredictable, that had to be propitiated and appeased at a heavy price. The institution of human sacrifice is a phenomenon curiously neglected by anthropologists, although it is found in every part of the world at the dawn of civilization and even at the height of pre-Columbian cultures. It is epitomized in one of the early chapters of Genesis, where Abraham prepares to cut the throat of his son out of sheer love of God. The ubiquity of human sacrifice is one of the earliest manifestations of the paranoid trend in the human psyche. The forms changed, but the trend persisted throughout the holy massacres of history, culminating in the genocidal enterprises of our time. Even the promise of eternal life was offered only to a small minority of mankind, at the price of eternal torment for the vast majority. Paradise was an exclusive country club, but the gates of hell were open to all.

There is of course a reverse side of the medal. Devotion is not always misguided: language produced the treasures in our libraries; the discovery of death is the foundation on which pyramids and cathedrals were built. However, we are now concerned not with the glory of man but his predicament, and today that is the more urgent subject; it has achieved an urgency as never before. History is accelerating at an unprecedented rate like the molecules of a liquid that is coming to the boil. The contemporary equivalent of the Writing on the Wall are the diagramatic charts of the exponential curves representing the various explosions that surround us: population explosion, knowledge explosion, communications explosion, and the explosion of explosive power. We have all seen these curves in learned magazines, but none of us has seen a curve representing progress in theoretical and applied ethics. The reason is presumably that there is no progress to report since the days when Buddha sat under the Banyan tree, waiting for his oxcart. In contrast to the exponential curve, which shows at first a slow, then an ever-steeper rise until it seems to rocket into the sky, the missing ethical curve would show a blurred, wavy line with inconclusive ups and downs, and never get off the ground. This contrast provides us with a simple overall view of our history; it reflects the consequences of the split mind.

This, in conclusion, brings us back to our starting point. Evolution proceeds by trial and error, so we ought not be surprised if it turned out that there is some construction fault in the circuitry that we carry inside our skulls that would explain the unholy mess we have made of our history. The ultimate cause may be the exceptionally rapid growth of the hominid brain in the course of the last half-million years—a phenomenon that seems to be unique in evolutionary history. The brain explosion in the second half of the Pleistocene seems also to have followed the exponential curve that has become so familiar to us—and there may be more than a superficial analogy here, as both curves reflect the phenomenon of the acceleration of history on different levels. But explosions rarely produce harmonious results, and the evidence seems to indicate that in our case the result is insufficient coordination between the phylogenetically old areas of the brain and the new, specifically human areas of the neocortex, which were superimposed on it with such unseemly haste. A distinguished neurophysiologist, Professor Paul MacLean, has coined the term "schizophysiology" for this disorderly state of affairs in our central nervous system. He describes it as "a dichotomy in the function of the phylogenetically old and new cortex that might account for differences between emotional and intellectual behaviour. While our intellectual functions are carried on in the newest and most highly developed part of the brain, our affective behaviour continues to be dominated by a relatively crude and primitive system, by archaic structures in the brain whose fundamental pattern has undergone but little change in the whole course of evolution, from mouse to man."

The consequences of this built-in schizophysiology range from so-called normal behavior, where emotional bias distorts our reasoning only within tolerable limits, through neurotic and psychotic disorder in the individual, to the collectively held beliefs in irrational causes to which we are emotionally committed in blind devotion and militant enthusiasm.

The question is, as Bertrand Russell once said, how to persuade humanity to acquiesce in its own survival. The thermonuclear reaction, once invented, cannot be disinvented, and the Pandora's boxes of biological warfare are just waiting to be opened. One cannot play Russian roulette for long. The biological evolution of man seems to have come to a standstill, at least since Cro-Magnon days; since we cannot in the foreseeable future expect a change in human nature to arise by a spontaneous mutation, our only hope seems to be to discover techniques that supplant biological evolution and provide a cure for our collective ailments. I believe that once man decides to take his fate into his own hands, that possibility will be within his reach. Allow me to close on this hopeful note, without attempting to specify the particular fields of contemporary research on which that hope is based.

ALTERNATIVE NEURAL PATHWAYS TO VIOLENCE
by Paul D. MacLean

Paul MacLean is chief of the section on Limbic Integration
and Behavior Laboratory of Neurophysiology, National
Institute of Mental Health, Bethesda, Maryland.

It is commonly assumed that the greatest problem presented by over-population is ensuring sufficient food. Experiments conducted by Dr. John Calhoun, however, suggest that psychopathology resulting from crowding may pose even greater problems. He constructed four connecting pens with skyscraper types of nesting boxes in which rats could form communities and reproduce themselves indefinitely with food always provided in abundance. The most significant outcome was the abnormal social behavior that developed. Mothers commonly failed to suckle and rear their young because of constant interruptions by intruding males and females. In the course of nursing, a neighbor would call or "the telephone would ring," and a mother would drop her pup and seem to forget where she had left it. The community developed a superfluity of males, and homosexuality became rampant. The increased number of social contacts from crowding resulted in constant fighting in which animals sometimes lost their tails. These few illustrations suggest a parallel to the parental neglect, juvenile delinquency and homosexuality occurring in our overpopulated cities.

Ethologists have emphasized that an animal requires a certain amount of territory around itself in which to carry on the sustaining activities of life. The amount required varies from species to species. Evidence is accumulating with respect to several animal species that aggressiveness increases with increasing density of population. Even the mild tempered rabbit becomes a killer when crowding becomes excessive. Recently in popular scientific writing it has been frequently stated that man is uncommonly aggressive, and he has been compared unfavorably with lower primates because of this and his propensity to kill. But the peaceful coexistence of sub-human primates in the wild is possibly attributable to an abundance of living space and food; under conditions of captivity, crowding has been observed to result in violent and deathly struggle. Among animals, however, it is usually not death from combat that reduces population density to tolerable levels. Rather, Nature appears to have ruled that aggression should take its toll indirectly through wasting disease and loss of fertility. Surpassing other animals in intelligence and inventiveness, man has found an additional solution: the use of weapons works more quickly and just as effectively.

The great concern at the present time, of course, is that his latest weapons are potentially too effective. As Arthur Koestler has remarked in his book *The Ghost in the Machine:* "Before the thermonuclear bomb, man had to live with the idea of death as an individual; from now onward, mankind has to live with the idea of its death as a species." Although man, as we shall see, shares with other mammals the same types of primitive neural mechanisms for ensuring survival through violent action, he has at the same time the largest brain development for their intelligent control.

There are those who argue that one has no right to apply behavioral observations on animals to human affairs, but it is to be emphasized that man has inherited the basic structure and organization of three brains, the two oldest of which are quite similar to those of animals. For purposes of discussion I refer to the three prototypes as reptilian, old mammalian and new mammalian. Despite their great differences in structure and chemistry all three brains must interconnect and function together. One might imagine that man's brain has evolved somewhat like a house to which wings and superstructure are added. The hierarchical superstructuring is schematized in Fig. 1 *(page 26)*. Man's brain of oldest heritage is basically reptilian. It forms the matrix of the brain stem and comprises much of the reticular system, midbrain and basal ganglia. The reptilian forebrain is characterized by greatly enlarged basal ganglia that resemble those of mammals.

But in contrast to mammals there is only an incipient cortex. The evolving old mammalian brain is distinctive because of a marked expansion of the primitive cortex that, as will be explained, is synonymous with the limbic cortex. Finally, there mushrooms late in evolution a

continued on page 28

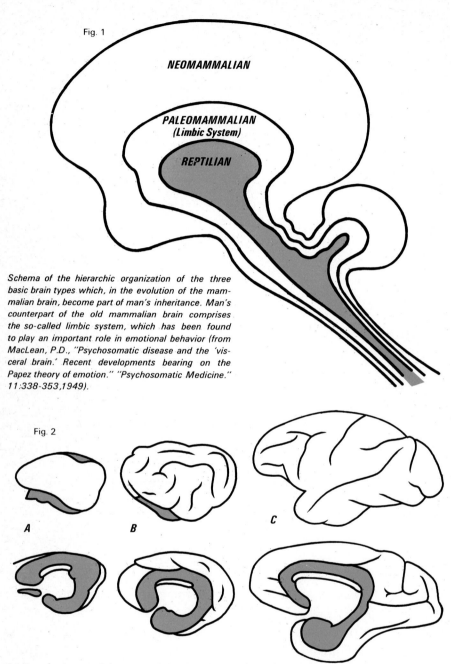

Fig. 1

NEOMAMMALIAN

PALEOMAMMALIAN
(Limbic System)

REPTILIAN

Schema of the hierarchic organization of the three basic brain types which, in the evolution of the mammalian brain, become part of man's inheritance. Man's counterpart of the old mammalian brain comprises the so-called limbic system, which has been found to play an important role in emotional behavior (from MacLean, P.D., "Psychosomatic disease and the 'visceral brain.' Recent developments bearing on the Papez theory of emotion." "Psychosomatic Medicine." 11:338-353,1949).

Fig. 2

A   B   C

In all mammals most of the cortex of the old mammalian brain (limbic system) is found in the great limbic lobe that surrounds the brain stem. These drawings, showing the relative sizes of the rabbit (A), cat (B) and monkey (C) brains, illustrate that throughout the mammalian series this lobe, represented in brown, forms a common denominator of the cerebrum. The neocortex, which mushrooms late in phylogeny, is shown in white (from MacLean, P.D., in: Wittkower, E. and Cleghorn, R., eds., "Recent Developments in Psychosomatic Medicine." London, Pitman, 1954).

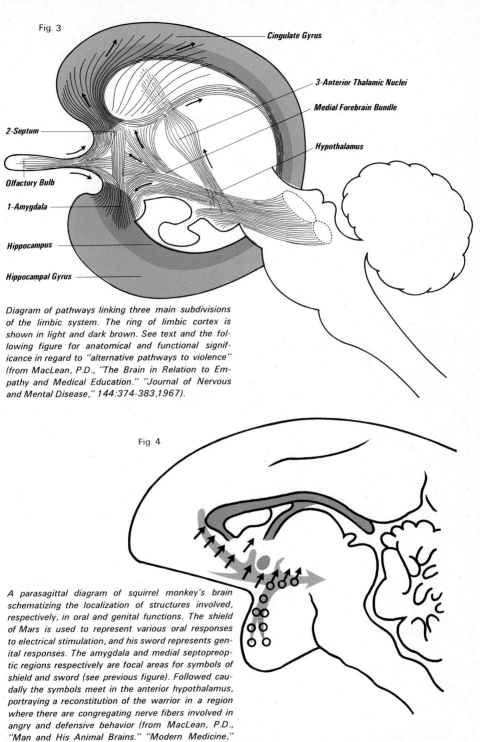

Fig. 3

Cingulate Gyrus

3-Anterior Thalamic Nuclei

Medial Forebrain Bundle

2-Septum

Hypothalamus

Olfactory Bulb

1-Amygdala

Hippocampus

Hippocampal Gyrus

Diagram of pathways linking three main subdivisions of the limbic system. The ring of limbic cortex is shown in light and dark brown. See text and the following figure for anatomical and functional significance in regard to "alternative pathways to violence" (from MacLean, P.D., "The Brain in Relation to Empathy and Medical Education." "Journal of Nervous and Mental Disease," 144:374-383,1967).

Fig. 4

A parasagittal diagram of squirrel monkey's brain schematizing the localization of structures involved, respectively, in oral and genital functions. The shield of Mars is used to represent various oral responses to electrical stimulation, and his sword represents genital responses. The amygdala and medial septopreoptic regions respectively are focal areas for symbols of shield and sword (see previous figure). Followed caudally the symbols meet in the anterior hypothalamus, portraying a reconstitution of the warrior in a region where there are congregating nerve fibers involved in angry and defensive behavior (from MacLean, P.D., "Man and His Animal Brains." "Modern Medicine," 32: 95-106,1964).

more complicated form of cortex called the neocortex, which is the hall-mark of the brains of higher mammals, and which culminates in man to become the brain of reading, writing and arithmetic.

In the popular language of today, the reptilian and old and new mammalian brains might be regarded as biological computers, each with its own subjective, gnostic, time-measuring, memory, motor and other functions. On the basis of the behavioral observations of ethologists, it might be inferred that the reptilian brain "programs" certain stereotyped behavior according to instructions based on ancestral learning and ancestral memories. In other words, it seems to play a primary role in instinctually determined functions such as establishing territory, finding shelter, hunting, homing, mating, breeding, forming social hierarchies, selecting leaders and the like. The British naturalist Eliot Howard emphasized that the establishment of territory may be an essential preliminary to mating and breeding.

The reptilian brain seems to be a slave to precedent. Having found a safe way home, for example, it is thereafter inclined to follow that route even though it means going around Robin Hood's barn. It would be satisfying to know to what extent the reptilian counterpart of man's brain determines his obeisance to precedent in ceremonial rituals, legal actions, political persuasions and religious convictions. In its stereotyped, obsessive, compulsive behavior it would seem as though the reptilian brain were neurosis bound by an ancestral superego. In any event, it appears to have inadequate machinery for learning to cope with new situations.

The evolutionary development in lower mammals of a respectable cortex might be regarded as Nature's attempt to provide the reptilian brain with a "thinking cap" and to emancipate it from the ancestral superego. In all mammals most of the primitive cortex is found in a ringlike convolution that Paul Broca called the limbic lobe because it surrounds the brain stem (limbic means "forming a border around"). From the standpoint of behavioral implications, it should be emphasized that this lobe, as illustrated in Fig. 2 *(page 26)*, is found as a common denominator in the brains of all mammals. This lobe, together with structures of the brain stem with which it has primary connections, is nowadays often referred to as the limbic system, terminology I suggested in 1952. Research of the last 25 years has shown that this old mammalian brain, once thought to be an olfactory brain, elaborates emotions that guide behavior with respect to the two basic life principles of self-preservation and the preservation of the species.

This old limbic cortex is basically primitive compared with the new cortex. From this it might be inferred that it continues to function at an animalistic level in animals as in man. Also, in marked contrast to the new cortex it has strong connections with the hypothalamus, which plays a basic role in integrating the performance of mechanisms involved in self-preservation and the preservation of the species.

In considering the topic of alternative neural pathways to violence we will need to refer to a simplified anatomical diagram of pathways linking three main subdivisions of the limbic system. Fig. 3 *(page 27)* focuses on three branchings of the large medial forebrain bundle that connects the ring of limbic cortex with the hypothalamus and reptilian counterparts of the brain stem. The two upper branches of this bundle meet with descending fibers from the olfactory apparatus and feed into the lower and upper halves of the ring through the amygdaloid nucleus and septum at the points marked No. 1 and No. 2. Clinical and experimental findings suggest that the lower part of the ring fed by the amygdala *(No. 1)* is primarily concerned with emotions and behavior that insure self-preservation. Its circuits are kept busy with the selfish demands of feeding, fighting and self-protection.

On the other hand, the pathway diverging to the septum *(No. 2)* and structures in the upper part of the ring appears to be involved in expressive and feeling states that are conducive to sociability and the preservation of the species. We have found, for example, that following electrical and chemical stimulation of parts of this circuit, male cats developed pleasure grooming and sexual reactions seen in courtship behavior. In the monkey we have worked out the cerebral representation of primitive sexual responses in considerable detail.

The close neural organization of oral and genital functions in this part of the limbic brain is presumably due to the olfactory sense that, dating far back in evolution, plays an important role in both feeding and mating. In the new brain the representation of the body is such that the head and tail stand at opposite poles like north and south. This is what one would expect of a structure with the nice discrimination of the new cortex. But in the limbic lobe, head and tail are brought into apposition by the olfactory sense. The persistence of this antique relationship in mammals makes it understandable that excitation in one structure readily spills over into the other so that sexual excitation may result in reflex mouthing and biting, and vice versa. Civilized man long suspected that the world was round before Columbus sailed to America. But how could he have imagined that the limbic lobe was a closed ring and that in "sailing" in one direction one would reach the head by way of the tail and vice versa?

It is relevant to sado-masochistic forms of behavior that pathways from the amygdala and septum involved respectively in oral and genital functions funnel into that same part of the hypothalamus that W. R. Hess and others have shown to be of central importance in angry and defensive behavior. In this region electrical stimulation at closely related points may cause penile erection, biting and signs of anger, fear or discomfort. Freud observed that "The sexually exciting influence of some painful affects such as fear, shuddering and horror is felt by a great many people throughout life and readily explains why so many seek opportunities to experience such sensations. . . ." He also remarked that "A number of persons report that they experienced the first signs of excitement in their genitals during fighting or wrestling with playmates. . . . The infantile connection between fighting and sexual excitement acts in many persons as a determinant for the future preferred course of their sexual impulse."

There is an old neurological adage that the head leads and the body follows. This would also be a figurative way of saying that self-preservation must come before the preservation of the species. Head and mouth spearhead the functions of destroying enemies or rivals and obtaining food for nourishment. Using the shield of Mars (O) as a symbol for responses involving the face and mouth, and his sword for genital responses (↗), one obtains an interesting picture in plotting the results of electrical stimulation of the brain on a diagram of the medial wall of the cerebrum. As illustrated in Fig. 4 (*page 27*), the symbols for mouth and face congregate in the region of the amygdala, while those for genital responses cluster in the region of the septum. In proceeding caudally, one sees a reconstitution of the warrior Mars (♂) in the anterior hypothalamus. Along the line of meeting of sword and shield is the region that is focal for congregating fibers involved in angry and defensive behavior. Since fighting is frequently a preliminary to mating as well as feeding, these findings suggest that Nature uses the same neural mechanisms for combat in both situations. Thus with respect to self-preservation and procreation there appear to be alternative neural pathways to violence.

The third pathway   The question arises as to how in primates the visual sense plays an increasingly important role in guiding socio-sexual behavior. This question turns our attention next to the third pathway in Fig. 3 (*page 27*), which bypasses the olfactory apparatus and connects the hypothalamus with the cingulate gyrus in the upper half of the ring. In evolution it is notable that the septal region in primates remains rather static whereas structures comprising this third subdivision of the limbic system become progressively larger and reach a maximum size in man. Some of our comparative brain and behavioral observations suggest that this condition reflects a shifting of emphasis from olfactory to visual influences in socio-sexual behavior. Significantly in this respect, stimulation within parts of this third subdivision, as in the septal circuit, elicits sexual responses in monkeys. We have found, on the other hand, that destruction of parts of this circuit may alter the genital display behavior of the small South American squirrel monkey. Our observations on this animal have revealed that it has a genital display that unlike the lemur, a more primitive primate, depends on visual rather than olfactory communication. This is confirmed by the finding that one variety of these monkeys will display equally well to its reflection in a mirror as to another monkey. In the communal situation the displaying animal vocalizes, spreads its thighs and directs the erect phallus toward the face of the other animal. Recalling what ethologists have described in reptilian and lower forms, the display in this monkey is the same in courtship as in the show of aggression. In the latter case the display is most dramatically seen when a new male is introduced into the territory of an established colony of monkeys. Within seconds all males begin to display with grinding teeth, and if the new monkey does not remain quiet and submissive with its head bowed, it is viciously attacked. In a special study, we found that the incidence of display among males provides a better measure of dominance than the outcome of rivalry for food.

Elsewhere I have discussed the comparative implications of these findings and have cited examples of remnants of genital display in man. In primitive cultures in different parts of the world the territorial aggressive implications of the display are illustrated by house guards—stone monuments showing an erect phallus—used to mark territorial boundaries. In Genesis, 24:2, Abraham says to his eldest servant, "Put I pray thee, thy hand under my thigh: And I will make thee swear . . . that thou shall not take a wife unto my son of the daughters of the Canaanites." Thigh, it is said, is used here euphemistically for the genitals. In his three contributions to the theory of sex, Freud commented: "The little child is above all shameless, and during its early years it evinces definite pleasure in displaying its body and especially its sexual organs." In the squirrel monkey, display may be triggered by the reflection of a single eye, suggesting that "looking into the eye" has primitive origins as an aggressive act. In Italy less than 200 years ago, amulets showing an erect phallus were worn as a protection against the evil eye.

Might it be inferred from these various observations on monkey and man that genital display and the impulse to mastery are built into the neural apparatus of the primate? I have suggested that primitive man may have learned that by covering himself he was able to reduce the unpleasant social tensions arising from the impulse to display, and this, rather than modesty, has led to the civilizing influence of clothing.

Thus far we have considered neural and behavioral findings that would appear to shed some light on observations that the acts of mastering, devouring and procreating seem to be inextricably connected. In concluding we have yet to consider a subject that goes to the roots of man's idealism—namely the close connection of sexuality and altruism. There is evidence that a concern for the welfare and preservation of the species is based on sexuality. It is a concern that leads to courtship and the rearing of a family. It is a concern that fosters education and the building of schools, libraries and museums. It is a concern that promotes "cultural grooming" in the form of art, music and architecture. It is a concern that inspires medical research to prevent suffering and dying of patients who have not yet become sick or old. It is a concern that has led man to think in terms of rockets, travel in outer space and the possibility of immortal life with the colonization of other worlds. It is possibly pertinent to the increasingly complicated socio-sexual behavior that one finds in ascending the phylogenetic scale of mammals, that the third subdivision of the limbic system connected by the third pathway shown in Fig. 3 (*page 27*) reaches a maximum size in man. This third subdivision is connected in turn with the forepart of our frontal lobes, a recent formation of the new cortex that culminates in man. Clinical analysis of cases with frontal lobe injury suggests that this new formation of the brain provides foresight in planning for ourselves and others. There is also evidence that it functions in helping us to gain insight into the feelings of others. Thus it would seem that "in the complex organization of the old and new structures under consideration, we presumably have a neural ladder, a visionary ladder, for ascending from the most primitive sexual feeling to the highest level of altruistic sentiments."

In the dawn's early light of brain research we gain the intimation that we have in the new brain a mechanism that is fully capable of dealing with the difficult medical and social problems of our time. The most explosive issue, of course, is the problem of controlling man's reptilian intolerance and reptilian struggle for territory, while at the same time finding a means of regulating our soaring population. Language barriers among nations present great difficulties in arriving at solutions. But the greatest language barrier lies between man and his animal brains; the neural machinery simply isn't there for communication in verbal terms. Nevertheless, in the last 2,000 years the layman all on his own has made great strides in domesticating his emotions. With the increasing insights that are being obtained from the brain and behavioral sciences, man should be able to continue to harness his emotions for progressively constructive purposes. If, through education, we could only apply what the brain already knows, the year 2000 might see the beginning of a truly golden age.

TOWARD THE STUDY OF VIOLENCE
by A. H. Maslow

A. H. Maslow is chairman of the Department of Psychology at Brandeis University and president of the American Psychological Association.

The most important thing to say at once is that we know—in the scientific sense—very little about violence, or any aspect of it. Since, like many others, I consider this kind of knowledge to be a necessary if not a sufficient condition for "curing" destructive violence, I would like to add my voice to the many others that are being raised to urge concerned intellectuals to help in this effort to advance knowledge. It is my firm opinion that good will, good intentions and good goals are in themselves often ineffective and even achieve the opposite of what they intend unless they are backed up with relevant facts.

Secondly I think I can contribute most usefully to this symposium by being personal. In 1941 I dedicated my life to helping to construct a "Psychology for the Peace Table." Indeed I had been preparing myself to write an encyclopedic book on aggression and hostility, destructive and constructive, by getting training in animal psychology, child psychology, psychoanalysis, social anthropology, endocrinology, constitutional biology and psychology, psychological and biological health and pathology, etc. At that time it was at least conceivable that one person could achieve this integration and "keep up" with all these fields of knowledge. Today of course it is absolutely impossible. Yet my conviction remains that these and more disciplines (e.g., history, politics, sociology, social philosophy, axiology) must be integrated if we are to understand violence well enough to manage it within the person, interpersonally, within the society and internationally.

I therefore propose that we turn to team research as a model in which a group of individuals, each trained well in one of these fields, works together as a research unit. One urgent job that could be done *only* by such a team would be producing a general handbook of the relevant knowledge already available. All the books on such subjects as aggression that are available today, in my opinion tend to overgeneralize from a single discipline, but they could become useful if integrated and fused in an overall vision.

First of all, I would stress the great importance of the fact that most kinds of psychotherapy are successful both in reducing the quantity of destructive hostility and also in changing its quality. I mean by the latter the change from cruelty, vindictiveness, sadism and destructiveness to indignation against injustice, to self-affirmation, to defending oneself against exploitation and the like. The lesson to be learned here is that violence has *two* antonyms, not just one. It can be *either* absence of violence or else it can be "healthy aggression" rather than unhealthy.

Another lesson from many kinds of depth psychotherapeutic experience, both with children and adults, is that one *always* finds some violent fantasies and impulses in *all* individuals (in our culture and possibly in all cultures) both justified (or healthy) and unjustified (or unhealthy), but that permission to accept and express these fantasies and thoughts verbally is often cathartically satisfying enough to lower greatly the probability of *acting* on these impulses. In general, this statement had better be called "agreed upon by the therapists"—that is by expert opinion—rather than verified fact. Much fruitful scientific work can be done in this area, especially in transforming, drawing from this general finding its educational applications, both in school, in the family and in other social institutions. It raises very clearly the possibility of bringing up children to *act* less violently without compromising healthy self-affirmation.

Direct study of psychologically healthy individuals confirms the foregoing conclusions: that one finds in them a lesser quantity of destructive impulses and behaviors; that these dreams, impulses and fantasies however never go to the zero point; and that healthy self-affirmation, protection of the self against injustice to self and others, etc., are always found in such individuals, i.e., they can be and are forceful and aggressive under certain circumstances. There are some indications that such healthy people may be more comfortable with and accepting of their own aggressive thoughts and (justified) actions, and feel less guilty about them than average people do.

There is still considerable confusion in the various scientific literatures of the intrapsychic, the interpersonal and the cultural and societal. It must be stressed that generalizing from one to the other is most frequently a mistake. So also is it dangerous to generalize from animal data to human conclusions. The human species has its own specific characteristics: chief among them is a considerable loss (or, at any rate weakening) of instinctive tendencies throughout the life of the individual. The consequence is that culture becomes extremely important in actualizing whatever hereditary and constitutional species-characteristics and potentialities the human baby is born with.

In this connection I have found extremely useful Ruth Benedict's concept of "synergy" and her comparisons of high and low synergy cultures, i.e., of "healthy" and "unhealthy" cultures. It is quite clear that societal arrangements in themselves can either foster or discourage violence. A purely intrapsychic, nonsocietal explanation of violence is certain to be limited or distorted or even idiotic. But so also is the purely sociological or economic or political explanation apt to look foolish to the psychologist, and to be very vulnerable to his criticisms. We now know enough to be sure that the mutual feedback relations between personality and culture are absolutely necessary in order to understand *either* personality *or* culture.

A great help toward understanding this interrelationship is a rapidly growing literature on organization theory, managerial theory and work psychology. Unfortunately this important work is not yet well enough known to a majority of social psychologists and social scientists in general. As an introduction to this body of knowledge, I would recommend the books referred to in my *Eupsychian Management: A Journal,* Irwin-Dorsey, 1965, and a new journal in which this kind of work is now published, *The Journal of Applied Behavioral Science.*

This literature also demonstrates clearly the societal and small group arrangements and techniques that encourage increase in violence or that discourage it and make it less likely to happen.

Finally, I would like to call attention to a finding in motivation psychology that I feel to be a great help to me in understanding the "hierarchy of violences" (*Eupsychian Management,* pages 236-246, "On Low Grumbles, High Grumbles and Metagrumbles"). Very briefly, my finding was that improving conditions leads only to *transient* happiness and contentment, which then usually gives way to a "higher" discontent. That is to say, we must expect discontent and grumbling as an intrinsic aspect of the human condition, along with the possibility of acting aggressively against the sources of discontent. But we can make a very fruitful distinction between the *quantity* of grumbling (which seems to tend toward constancy no matter *how* good the social environment), and on the other hand, the quality or level of discontent that gets "higher" as social conditions improve. That is to say, people will then complain and be aggressive about justice, truth, beauty and the like, rather than about food, shelter or danger to life. Improving society, though it cannot be expected to abolish discontent, can lift this discontent and aggressiveness from the selfish to the unselfish, from the purely personal to the more altruistic and brotherly, and from low aspirations to high aspirations not only for oneself but for others and for the world.

SYMBOLS, LANGUAGE AND HUMAN VIOLENCE
by C. H. Waddington

C. H. Waddington is Professor of Animal Genetics, University of Edinburgh, Scotland, and author of *Introduction to Modern Genetics, Ethical Animal, Nature of Life* and *Biology for the Modern World.*

The violence of the human species has two main roots. The less important is the tendency to enjoy bursts of intense physical effort, which man shares with other higher animals whose livelihood depends in any important way on hunting. This desire for violent exercise, usually accompanied by excitement, would almost certainly have been built deep into man's genetic endowment by the processes of natural selection. But it is combined with another and more important "tendency to violence," which is not derived from the action of natural selection but is connected with the very means by which man has transcended, and largely escaped from, the forces of merely biological evolution. Man has developed, to a pitch of efficiency of a different order to anything found in other animals, a system of symbolic communication and conceptual thought that enables him to transmit information from one generation to the next by means that operate much more quickly and subtly than the biological genetic mechanism on which most living things rely. But symbolic transmission (language) requires that *meaning* should be attached to essentially non-significant symbols (sound = words; marks = writing). As I have argued at length elsewhere (*The Ethical Animal,* Atheneum, 1961), the process by which the young human infant is brought to realize that certain sounds are symbols conveying conceptual meanings involves the exertion of parental or quasi-parental authority to restrain the freedom of the infant's action or to deny the satisfaction of its needs. This authority will be to some extent accepted, and to some extent resented and opposed. This provides the most important basic root from which arises most human violence, not only in infancy but throughout life.

The "hunting adventure" type of violence in man is of comparatively little importance. It is, as we have seen, probably a built-in characteristic, and as such needs satisfying, but this can be done—or could be done—with relatively little planning of social developments in such forms as football, motor racing, fox hunting or similar sports. The dangerous forms of violence are those involving meaning. It is useful to consider them as of two contrasting kinds; one in which violence occurs because too much meaning is attached to some set of concepts, while in the other people become violent as a protest against their inability to discover enough meaning in their surroundings. In general, wars conducted by whole societies fall into the first category, being motivated by beliefs of a religious, political or racial kind; the apparently motiveless thuggery and mugging of our big cities, or the excessive violence of gangster competitiveness, are examples of the second kind. But, as usual in real-life situations, these neat categories are often mixed up in practice; the violence of the German Nazis, for instance, was only partly based on beliefs in racial and political meanings and had within it a strong element of aggression derived from a failure to find adequate meaningfulness in ordinary-life situations.

What we need to do in connection with violence derived from lack of meaning is not, I think, to find substitutes for it, but to create a social system in which a feeling of an absence of meaning does not arise. This means nothing less than the recreation of a sense of purpose throughout the whole of society. This purpose need not be explicitly religious, but I doubt if, at least in the developed world, it can be wholly in the realm of material economics (though that may supply a powerful enough force for the developing world for a generation or two).

How to control violence due to excessive belief in some system of meanings is the most difficult problem. Part of the answer may be to reduce the rewards that could be won or the losses that could be sustained. In a sufficiently affluent society, in which the upper limit of wealth was controlled as well as the lower, gangster violence for gain would lose much of its point. On the international scale, the nuclear balance of terror depends on the conviction of the nuclear powers that they could not in practice gain very much from attacking their enemies, since they would themselves be attacked in their turn. But it seems probable that such rational controls will not be enough in themselves. They need to be supplemented in three ways. Firstly, by persuading people that there are other, nonviolent methods by which they can achieve their aims, e.g., by Gandhian tactics. Secondly, by letting them feel they can work off their aggression through methods of this kind with as much internal satisfaction as they would get from shooting people with bullets —Gandhi was a saint, but he was also as bloody-minded as they come and certainly enjoyed making himself detested by his enemies. Finally, I feel that steps will have to be taken, particularly in the earliest stages of education, to try to reduce the amount of meaningfulness that people attach to symbols to no more than that which is necessary for them to be symbols, or as near to that ideal as we can get.

VIOLENCE AND ALIENATION
Adapted from the 1968 commencement address at Santa Clara University.
by Morris L. West

Morris West is an Australian playwright and the author of *The Shoes of the Fisherman* and *The Devil's Advocate*.

The Oxford Dictionary defines alienation as "estrangement, diversion to a different purpose . . . insanity." It is a significant juxtaposition . . . estrangement, diversion to a different purpose, insanity. It implies a connection between three states—a consequential deterioration. It hints at morbidity—disease—a disease special to the human animal.

First, he discovers himself a stranger, disconnected from the group in which he lives. Next, he finds himself committed to purposes in contradiction to the purposes of the group. Finally, he cuts himself off from it, either by an act of hostility or by an act of flight, that the alienists, those who deal with sick minds, call fugue. In our time, and in many countries of the world, the sickness has become epidemic. We have entered the age of the aliens.

In a very real sense, it is the plague of the 20th Century, as the Black Death was the plague of medieval Europe. Like all plagues, it induces terror, disorder, violence, quackery, fanaticism. These are social ills, too; they are related to but not identical with the original disease. They arise from it; they may lead back to it; but in the beginning they are not the same.

So, let us try to define a little more closely. A nonconformist is not necessarily an alien. I define a nonconformist as one with a healthy disrespect for certain aspects of his society—for its false values, for its magical formulas, for its outworn rituals, for its creaking mechanisms. He may be and generally is a very healthy member of the group.

A protester is not necessarily an alien. He may be and often is a physician for the ills of the body corporate. A revolutionary is not necessarily an alien. There are those who wish to contrive a constructive change, which is a healthy and necessary action upon human history. On the other hand, he may be a destructor; in this case there is a pathological aspect to his activity. The true alien, the irrevocably estranged, is one who, by fugue or violence, disconnects himself from rational life and from the human community that, however imperfect its social structures, is still a guardian of human rationality, human dignity and human security. What produces this disease of alienation?

In this short space, I can only point to certain possible causes, to propose them for your meditation. The function of the healer does not belong exclusively to the physician, the surgeon, the psychiatrist. There are not enough of these experts to deal with the manifold ills of the world. The function devolves upon us all. If we do not perform it, we shall commit ourselves into the hands of the quacks and the fanatics, who truly are destroyers, infected with the same disease that they pretend to cure.

Estrangement always begins with violence—a physical or psychic violence, done to a human creature at a time when he cannot protect himself against it. The violence produces a wound or trauma. The trauma produces a disfunction that continues to exaggerate itself through the whole course of a human life.

The wound may be inflicted by an individual—by an act of terror or brutality, by the deprivation of love, which is the only support of a child in the period of its nurture. It may be inflicted by society itself, by racial or religious discrimination, by the break-up of a family unit, by intolerable poverty, by direct injustice, by a theft of opportunity, by a whole gamut of cruel invasions, from the bullying of a child in the school yard to the monstrous holocausts of the concentration camps. The trauma may be inflicted impersonally, by the very condition of society itself.

The industrial revolution has thrown up great ant-heap cities, in which the links of family and tribe and community are quickly broken, in which people are thrust into abrasive contact with their fellows and, at the same time, into a reactive isolation from them. The contact produces frustration, mistrust, fear, a brute competition for elbow room and opportunity. The isolation compounds the frustration, turns the fear into nightmare and the competitive drive into outright hostility. In the mass, man feels himself naked and de-humanized. After a while, his fellows lose their faces and become unhuman. In the extreme, the wounded one finds no one to whom he can turn for help. He finds no one on whom he can focus a self-healing and other-healing love. In the extreme, he can find no redress against the injustice inflicted by a faceless multitude. So, he may personify a multitude in one person and against that one person wreak a pathological revenge by assault, murder or assassination.

Modern communications compound the pathology. The madness spreads like the dancing madness of the middle ages in Europe. The violence depicted upon our television screens suggests and provokes an answering violence. The anarchist begets the dehumanized riot policeman, dressed like a man from outer space. The conspirator begets the torturer; the torturer begets the conspirator. The multitude spawns the outlaw. The outlaw unites the multitude in a mindless fury against its own victim. The madness is cyclic—a saw-toothed wheel, spinning

ever-faster and faster, until it explodes, splintering itself and frag-
menting human society at the same time. I believe, and I think most
of you believe, that we are very close to this fragmentation point now.
What can we do to hold it off? What can we do to slow down the wild
spinning, to stop the mad dance of death, into which we are all being
drawn, willy-nilly?

More deaths will not do it. Guns and truncheons and antiriot devices will not do it. Communicators can help, by a deliberate and
concerted effort to damp down incitements to violence—at whatever
cost to their circulations. Educators can do it, by a deliberate and concerted effort to infuse into their teaching an inter-personal relationship
of tolerance and patience with diversity, a sense of mutual responsibility.

In all too many of our universities, the watchword of the cynics is,
"Publish or perish." We had better begin teaching the things that are essential to our peace, otherwise we shall all perish. Every class and
group in society can provide its own palliative to violence, but only
the whole organism, working together, can cure the basic sickness of
alienation. The sickness is in the bloodstream, not in the cut finger or
the bloody head. And the bloodstream must deplete itself for a while,
to fight the infection. Society must spend itself to survive. We cannot
maintain an economy of waste while there are hungry people three
blocks away. We cannot walk secure in the streets where there are work-
less men. We cannot expect a civilized response from those who are
denied a civilizing influence of education and equality. We cannot expect to sleep safe when any unhappy and disordered person can get a
gun for the price of a mail-order subscription. We will never stop shooting until we understand that the face we have lined up in our sights,
black, white or yellow, is our own face, and that every invasion of the
rights of our fellowmen is an act of suicide.

THE U.S.A.—A CASE STUDY

A MORAL EQUIVALENT FOR RIOTS

by Harvey Wheeler

Harvey Wheeler, former professor of political science at Washington and Lee University, is a fellow at the Center for the Study of Democratic Institutions and co-author of *Fail-Safe*.

In 1967, Malcolm Moos, who became President of the University of Minnesota but who was then an executive at the Ford Foundation, asked me to make a general investigation into the topic of violence. I must explain that I had not previously engaged in any special studies qualifying me as an expert in this field, but perhaps Moos felt this was in my favor. At least I had no preconceptions or predispositions toward one or another of the various contending schools of thought.

The first request I made was to be allowed to interpret the subject broadly. I did not want to look solely into the subject of race riots—though obviously this would be one of the chief problems I wanted to be able to say something about in the end. Initially, however, I wanted to find out about all sorts of violence: sporadic acts of violence by assassins or snipers, such as that of the berserk student who mounted the tower at the University of Texas and shot down at people right and left; violence of student demonstrators, both those directed against their universities and those directed against their nation's war; the hippies, who in one sense are waging a violent attack on the conventional morality of the established culture. Finally, I wanted to study the various national liberation movements found among the peoples of the third world.

I was given complete freedom to decide where to go, whom to seek out and how to prepare the study. So I packed my tape recorder—and my wife—and off we went, to Los Angeles, to Stanford, to Berkeley, Harvard, North Carolina, New York, London, Paris, Geneva and many other places. I talked to famous leaders of the civil rights movement and to infamous leaders of street gangs; to philosophers, psychologists, sociologists, political scientists, reporters, public officials, etc. In all, I taped over 100 hours of interviews. And my wife, who sat in on most of them, required nearly a year to complete the transcriptions. It has been a terribly tedious task because the interviews were conducted under the most trying circumstances: in hotel rooms, at a street corner, in ghetto homes—with children, neighbors and even street runners, dashing in and out constantly. In bars, in ghetto bars and in the bar of the London Hilton. In offices, and even in cars. And while ever since then I have pondered these interviews, and the problems revealed by them, this is the first time I've been able to try to put them all together to see if there are reliable conclusions and recommendations that can be derived from them.

First, I would like to give a brief summary of the theories and suggestions about violence made by my respondents.

(1) In the first place, most of them agreed that violence itself is not the thing to look at if one wants to understand it. That is, violence is a symptom rather than a cause, and if one wishes to reduce violence it will be of little avail to attack it directly, as if it, violence, were something that could be cured or eliminated, head on. Rather, one must try to get at the underlying causes or roots of what elicits violence.

(2) Next, most people, in one way or another, believe violence to be an indelible part of human nature in some fundamental way. This opinion brought together such otherwise diverse respondents as Hans J. Morgenthau and Martin Luther King. So it is not possible, or even desirable, for us ever to achieve the complete elimination of violence. Rather, we may eliminate some of its most destructive manifestations. And perhaps we may divert it into rather more harmless, or even constructive channels.

(3) There was a tendency to point out that all societies are violent, and America is especially so. However, societies draw lines between what they consider "good" violence and "bad" violence. Many southern whites, for example, consider violence against Negroes to be a good thing. Many of those interviewed about Martin Luther King's assassination clearly betrayed the feeling that it was probably a good thing

that he was shot. And I must relate that a close relative, who lives in Indiana, but was born (as I was) in Waco, Texas, called me the day after the assassination to ask my opinion about it, stating that he thought of it as a "blessing." Now this is really a horrifying thought, but it is a thought that is harbored in the breasts of a large number of Americans, and we must face that fact. The Kerner Commission, remember, referred to the root of the problem as lying in a deep-seated racism that permeates American society. This is something most of my respondents assented to. So the problem of distinguishing violence is difficult. We officially approve of search-and-destroy violence in the Vietnam war. We approvingly portray the battlefield results of this policy on television each evening at the "happy hour." Recall the ghastly scenes of on-the-spot executions and the famous cigarette lighter incident that caused the expulsion of a network reporter because he filmed a GI setting fire to native homes. Recall again, that in *most* states we retain the death penalty. But more insidious is the kind of permissive violence that we are scarcely aware of. Negroes are aware of it, however, for it strikes against them daily. Take the example of a policeman executing a death sentence on his own initiative. A youth is caught in the act of stealing a watch through a smashed store window. The officer shouts for him to stand still. The youth panics and runs. The officer shoots him dead. Or the joy-rider who has pinched a car to drive until the gas is gone. A patrol car detects him, gives chase and literally drives the boy on until he smashes himself to death in an accident. So there is violence that runs throughout society—every society—and only some of it is really called "violence" and bemoaned as such.

(4) One of my respondents referred to this as the problem, not of violence, but of "violation." Violence, he said, must be looked at in terms of the violation of the dignity of human beings. In those terms, violence is merely the sporadic counter-response that breaks out when one's humanity and one's dignity have been violated. So a culture in which human relationships are characterized by a great deal of violation will be a culture producing a great deal of counter-violence. America, as Dr. Edward Lurie has shown, has been a personality-

violating culture since its birth. It has been unable to solve any of its greatest collective or internal problems without resorting to violence. Aside from that, however, new cultural forces associated with the scientific revolution and with bureaucratization carry a special kind of violation all their own. And as these technological and organizational varieties of violation have increased, so has the incidence of counterviolation. Again, this more or less impersonal, or "systemic" violation, helps account for the more or less impersonal, or "antisystem" violence of the reactions, as when snipers choose expressway autos as random targets; as when rioters attack, not other races or even other people, but symbols of the system that violates them. This is the meaning of looting.

(5) This brings us to another, generally agreed to proposition. Again, it is a generalization about American history. After the Civil War, America gave verbal, statutory and even constitutional expression to the principle of equal rights for Negroes; but at the same time it instituted an informal (in the South, quite formalized) racist culture in which Jim Crow regulations and practices of a most degrading (violating) type were enforced generally throughout the country. We tend to think of Jim Crow as a Southern institution, but in the North it often had an even more cruel impact than in the South.

The lovely little Northern town—let us call it "Elmstown"—where I grew up had two Negro families. One was headed by the kindly old "handkerchiefhead darkey" who was barber at the Elks Club, the other by a lady, apparently quite gracious, who served the community otherwise. This was degrading enough, but the reason only two families lived there was that the town had earlier chased all the others out, posting signs at each road entering the town reading "NIGGER, DON'T LET THE SUN GO DOWN ON YOU IN ELMSTOWN." In northern cities, of course, the pattern of ghettoization—completely unknown at that time in southern cities—was rigidly enforced.

The result of this uniform human violation was the creation of the myth of Negro inferiority. And that myth was accepted, with very few exceptions, by Negroes themselves. In short, Negroes believed they were as inferior as white men said they were, and this official violation of their humanity was turned inward, upon themselves, leading them to hate themselves and their blackness and their negroid characteristics. They valued light skins over dark and violated their own natures—as in hair straighteners—in a perpetual effort to suppress their negritude. Amos and Andy, Stepin Fetchit, Rochester—white man's stereotypes of the good but slavish darkey—were actually accepted by them as their heroes. The result of this inward turning of violence against themselves was the destruction of any possibility of an integral family structure. Negro women led all others in depreciating their men, contributing to the so-called "emasculation" of the Negro male about which we have heard so much. And this internalization of violence, when it spilled out, took the form of actual physical violence against each other in the highly-publicized brawls, cuttings and wife-beatings that authorities reinforced by applying different law-enforcement standards for Negroes. Negroes were overpoliced in their relations to property and to whites; they were underpoliced in their relations to each other. It was all right for Negroes to knife one another to death—they were "animals" and the fewer of them the better. But it was in effect a capital offense to even mildly affront a white. In short, Negroes not only internalized violence, taking it out on each other, they were "paid off" for doing so by the larger society. But the change came after the 1954 Supreme Court decision on school segregation. Then, for the first time, Negroes began to turn violence outward against the white society that had violated them. First in the sit-ins and demonstrations; later in the riots. And the result of this was a rebirth, or perhaps an inauguration, of Negro self-respect. This has been the psychic power of the recent pattern of violence. It has been an assertion of self-respect. For the first time Negro women and children looked up to their men *because* of their manhood. For the men, the change is heady stuff. Once tasted it is not easily turned away from.

(6) Out of this grows a related factor. It has been said that America has had the tradition of solving its problems through violence. Daniel Bell, a sociologist, has written of an interesting variant of this tradi-

tion of violence in "Crime as an American Way of Life." Bell pointed out that the white, Anglo-Saxon Protestant got here first and monopolized all the official avenues to wealth and status. Then came the immigration waves: Irish, middle Europeans, Jews, etc. Each was faced with a foreclosure of the normal avenues of participation in the bourgeois bounties of the land. The Irish turned to politics and monopolized the party system, using it to gain not only office, but systematizing graft into a characteristically American kind of capital accumulation. When the middle Europeans arrived later, not only business, but also politics, was closed to them. The result, says Bell, was a resort to crime as "an American Way of Life": crime as a way of becoming middle class Americans; and so on for other groups. But what of the Negro? Now we must consider the possibility that violence —direct action in the streets—has become the Negro version of this pattern of Americanization. All other avenues are closed; only direct action, sometimes issuing in violence, is left. This is the historic setting within which the Black Power movement must be understood. And that being so, one must also look forward to the possibility that rioting and street demonstrations will become the institutionalized form of Americanization for Negroes. I suspect we are witnessing the confirmation of this new institution today in the canonization of Martin Luther King Jr.

(7) We conclude that there is a large measure of truth to the Black Power charge that America is an imperialist culture. The imperialism with which America approaches the world outside is mirrored by a related form of imperialism that it turns against its own ethnic minorities. Thus arises the charge that the Negro (and the Mexican-American, and others) lives in a colonial status in his own country. The rather transparent validity of this charge is what forges unity between the struggle of the Negro against domestic oppression and the international struggles of the third world against colonialism. Both are essentially anti-imperialist movements and both will have to apply generally similar tactics to achieve their goals. This does not *necessarily* mean violent tactics, but all of us know that the situation at home and

abroad is fraught with a very high violence-potential. This is also why Coretta King was right, two years ago, when she finally convinced Martin that the struggle in America would have to be linked with the struggle against American imperialism abroad.

All this is plain enough, but what is the source of this domestic imperialism of ours? The Kerner Commission is right as far as it goes. America *is* a racist culture. But the Kerner Commission doesn't go nearly far enough. Our internal form of despotism begins innocuously, right at birth. The medical evidence is mounting that children who begin life in conditions of emotional and nutritional deprivation develop physical and mental deficiencies that are virtually irreversible, no matter how healthful their conditions may later become. Now of course, this is a condition that afflicts *all* the poor. But because of the proportional overconcentration of Negroes in the so-called culture of poverty, the effects of deprivation strike selectively against them. So they start life with ineradicable chains dragging down their every step. But even if it were eliminated overnight, another cultural barrier still lies in their path, and it will prove to be the most difficult one to eradicate. This has to do with the acculturation process and with the way it relates to the educational process. We know that the performance of children in schools is directly correlated with the cultural and economic status of their parents. Children from highly educated affluent homes will inevitably make better grades, go to better schools, acquire higher degrees and ultimately find better jobs, than those from deprived homes. It is sometimes falsely concluded that this means that education is the bootstrap by which all can pull themselves out of deprivation into white middle-class society. But that is transparently false, is it not? One has to *be* middle class to *start* with, in order to be middle class at the end. Education as such has little or nothing to do with it. Now the other side of this is that deprived boys and girls, starting in school, have no cultural reinforcement at home. They have no stimulus urging them toward cultural heights. They have limited verbal and reading skills to reinforce their schoolroom efforts. As a result they automatically get processed through what we call the "track" system, and what the English call "streaming." The track system means that even in schools that are technically desegregated, there is an internal segregation based upon test performance. Test performance is sometimes thought to represent innate intellectual ability. In fact, however, intelligence tests merely represent the conditions of one's cultural origins. So, those from culturally deprived homes are automatically passed through the grades, regardless of performance, until legal school-leaving age is reached. At that time they are dumped out on the streets, where they will spend the rest of their lives grubbing for existence. The second track is for those with low, but passable achievement records. They are placed in the manual arts, nonacademic track and are destined for the menial, semi-skilled trades. The highest, of course, are put into the liberal arts, college preparatory programs and they inevitably will end up with college degrees and Establishment jobs. Now the point is that the track system reinforces, and even magnifies, the initial condition with which students begin life. Before a child is 10 years old the school system has already *determined*, beyond his ability to influence it, the entire lifetime career of the individual. Of course, there are a few extremely rare cases in which the pattern is overcome. And we paternalistically display these with a great show of pride. This is the cruelest cultural despotism imaginable. It is also remorselessly violent. For who can argue with objective placement tests? So what to do about it? Shouldn't any sensible child—or any sensible high-school student—when faced from the beginning of life with a predetermined second-class status, destined to last forever, react with violence to this ultimate violation of his innate talents?

(8) An aspect of this same kind of despotism reaches even to proper middle-class children. Our culture has always been goaded by the whiplash of the dollar. The threat of economic failure (absolute or relative) dogs our steps from birth to death. And this is a violence that often becomes too much even for the seemingly well-to-do. But recently the whiplash of the dollar has become supplemented by that of the school. For *each* person's status, rich as well as poor, appears to depend upon his grade records. So the grade record becomes the whiplash

of the young, terrorizing them from kindergarten on. And where the school stops, the parent takes up. Every day each middle-class child is hounded as he returns home from school as mom and dad conduct a third-degree interrogation on how well he performed (meaning how high his grades were) at school that day. So school itself (abetted by career-conscious parents) becomes a place of violence and terror whose whiplash is the grade system that reaches an apex for the hardy in the ultimate indignity of the College Board exams.

Now the answer to one of our preliminary questions begins to reveal itself. We saw that Coretta King was right in associating the plight of the American Negro with that of the world's colonial peoples. And now it is apparent that the systematic "violation" of our youth brings Negroes, hippies and university students together into the same framework in the same cause.

(9) It was often remarked, before Watts, that Los Angeles was the most unlikely place for a riot to occur. Watts is not a ghetto in the normal sense of the word. It abounds with single-family homes. I remember in the 1950s hearing Eastern Negroes say that Los Angeles was the Negro's "heaven"; "Man, *that*'s where I want to go when I die." A second comment about Watts was that it was not technically a "race riot." It was not against whites, at least, not personally. So, Watts was the most affluent Negro community in the world, and its riot was directed against *that* very community. How can we explain this? There is general agreement that the Watts pattern fits well into what is known about *all* the revolutions of history. They do not start among those making up the dregs of society. Moreover, they do not occur when oppression and exploitation are at their worst. So-called "revolutions of the belly" are statistically rare in history, and when they occur they usually have little effect on the conditions of those in revolt —except death. Rather, revolutions typically occur among those who have experienced a definite, steady rise in their conditions of life, and *then* suffer a setback. Revolutions are made by rising classes rather than by declining classes. And this leads us to the current catch phrase about the "revolutions of rising expectations," that is, the rev-

olutions being carried out by all peoples in the world today who want to enjoy the good things in life made famous by Americans. There is general agreement that the Negro Revolution is another one of these revolutions of rising expectations. It is precisely because Negroes desperately want to enjoy the beneficences of the American way of life that they are in revolt. It is LIFE magazine, actively abetted by *Ebony* magazine, and multiplied a thousand-fold by television commercials, that provides the real stimulus to the Negro Revolution. And this is one reason why the revolts take the form of burning and looting. Revolutions destroy the physical symbols of deprivation; in the present case these are tenement houses and gouging merchants. And then the rebels go on to looting, helping themselves to the gadgets and goodies the mass media have overstimulated them to desire.

(10) Finally, there appears to be irrefutable physiological and anthropological evidence that the mere fact of physical overcrowding induces violence. Some anthropologists claim to be able to chart reliable curves of violence-potentials correlated with rates of congestion. Dramatic confirmation comes from experiments with chimpanzees. Chimps are normally quite peaceful creatures. At the most they engage in their curious ritualized shouting wars in which violence seldom, if ever, results. In one experiment a collection of chimps was loaded on a ship for transportation to an uninhabited Caribbean island—as an experimental refuge. During the period of shipboard crowding, they developed on their own most of the typical maladies of human beings. They learned how to fight each other, even to death. They acquired coronary problems and they developed a full range of mental diseases. But what is worse, once learned on shipboard, their violent patterns of behavior were continued even after debarkation on an island where sufficient space and food could have permitted the return to their traditional (presumably instinctual) ways of peace.

It is apparent from these 10 general propositions about violence that the problem runs quite deep—so deep that not even massive investments in the improvement of the physical conditions of the ghettos will resolve them. However, there are a few propositions that can be derived from what we have uncovered.

All of us have a new kind of awareness of violence. Indeed, our very outcry against it makes us appear as if we thought it never before had existed. The public astonishment being expressed today must be attributed to the fact that most *proper* Americans had grown secure in the belief that violence would never touch them. Violence was like rickets and scrofula—something found only in the underworld and the slums. So the novelty of today's violence is that it has spread out of the underworld and the ghettos into the everyday consciousness of the middle-class American suburbanite.

One possibly beneficial consequence of this novel awareness of violence middle-class whites are beginning to acquire is that, in an ironic way, it permits them to share an experience with Negroes previously denied them. Because one of the characteristics of the ghetto, a feature of its prevailing "weather condition" so to speak, is the omnipresence of violence. Violence is an everyday and every-moment feature of the "quality of life" in the ghetto. So in spite of all the tragic experiences we are undergoing in this time of violence, there is a sense in which it presents us with a perverse kind of cultural "enrichment." It permits us, in a way that nothing else could, to understand a very important fact about the condition of life that besets the Negro.

But, as we have seen earlier, violence has many faces. It is not only what blacks do when they riot, nor only what assassins do when they gun down a prominent leader. It is also the sporadic, anonymous act—it is a student in a university tower casually picking off passers-by far below; it is the hillside sniper taking random shots at freeway motorists; it is the casual seriatim murder of a chance collection of student nurses. And it is also university guerrillas marching under the banner of Che and Mao. Can we legitimately lump together all these diverse forms of violence and derive from them a deeper understanding of its nature?

The first thing to do is to refer to our earlier discussion about the distinction societies make between "good and bad" violence. This is something most of us seldom face. What we normally *call* violence is only "bad" violence. Accordingly, we tend to think of violence as being depraved or irrational. We seldom consider, for example, that acts of violence may be completely rational under certain circumstances. It does not automatically follow that because someone has engaged in an act of violence he is just a crazy kook. The point to be underscored is that all societies are violent societies. Our historians may be able to prove that America has been a little bit more violent than most other societies, but this must not be allowed to obscure the fact that in general violence has been the rule of history. Not only is it true that all societies are violent, it is also true that all societies possess "official," as well as "unofficial" forms of violence. It is only the unofficial forms of violence that history's proper people have bemoaned.

Consider the violence of an assassination. This is something we all find repellent, at first thought. If we look a bit deeper into ourselves, however, we find a confusion of emotions. Suppose one of the assassination attempts against Hitler had succeeded? Would not most of us have applauded the event wholeheartedly? But this, we hasten to reply, is "different." Besides, it is not valid to cite the case of Hitler because he was such an evil man. But then we must ask ourselves: can there be such a thing as a "just" assassination of evil men, as some philosophers claim there can be such a thing as a just war? And whose judgment of "evil men" do we accept?

In the widely televised interviews with Southerners at the time of Martin Luther King's assassination, not a few of them calmly discussed their sympathetic attitudes: it may have been for the best; or he got what was coming to him; or he had only reaped what he had sown; or that it was only unfortunate it had to happen in Memphis instead of somewhere else. With horror we came to realize the extent to which a sizable number of Americans really approved of the assassination. For them it was, in effect, a socially acceptable act. The same assassination was "good" violence for some and tragically "bad" violence for others. Something like this usually turns out to be true, in varying degrees, of all acts of violence, especially in societies undergoing very fundamental social transitions. In such societies—our own is one—the incidence of violence expands considerably. Moreover, the confusion of "good" and "bad" violence is considerably heightened; and with this grows confusion about its good and bad forms. It becomes more and more difficult to tell where a person stands, or ought to stand, with regard to violence, for such times force everyone to choose sides.

Recently, the Center for the Study of Democratic Institutions held a conference between Christians and Marxists in an effort to expand the so-called "East-West Dialogue." It was attended primarily by Eastern European Marxists (Communists) and Eastern European theologians. The theologians made the most radical point about violence. It was they who explained that as theologians, and as believing Christians, they would defend revolutionary violence in today's world. Their reasoning was simple. In their judgment, established society was everywhere more violent by far, and more evil by far, than were the protest movements organizing to overthrow it. They concluded that the incidental violence that might, in some cases, accompany those revolutionary movements, represented a far lesser and indeed more virtuous form of violence because of the much greater evil of that which they sought to abolish. We must conclude from the way people act and judge, that there are many contexts in which violence is regarded as justifiable. Even in individual cases there are many conditions under which we might not consider a specific act of violence to be irrational or bad.

When we speak of a time of rapid transition, what we really mean is that it is a time of revolution. And that indeed seems to be true of our own times. There are many ways of talking about this revolution. We speak of the scientific revolution, which I believe to be the most profound revolution this human race has known since the industrial revolution. It is a movement—a massive institutional development—of exactly the same order of seriousness as that which was introduced by the industrial revolution. Such massive revolutionary transitions are almost always accompanied by violence. One of these contemporary transitional conflicts is what we call the Cold War. The Cold War did not result from President Truman's irritability that grim morning in

Washington when Molotov stopped at the White House on his way to the charter meeting of the United Nations. Rather the Cold War seems to be best understood as the mode of violence the world is undergoing in its struggle to dissolve the nation-state system and to discover the outlines of the new forms of political order that are going to replace it. If this is so, the Cold War will not disappear until the nation-state system has been brought to an end. This in turn means that we are destined to experience various new phases of Cold War violence for a very long time yet. However, the rate of change appears to be accelerating every day and the nation-state may wither away much more rapidly than now seems imaginable.

History's most fundamental revolutions occur first in peoples' minds, and only after that are they acted out in institutions. Such a revolution is occurring in the world's mind right now. Many nations seem on the verge of splitting apart. Ethnic minorities are demanding autonomy throughout the world. A recent book tells us that Ukrainian nationalism is still very much alive in Russia, to say nothing of the Jewish problem. Everywhere such "self-strengthening" movements are making themselves felt and insisting upon recognition. At one time—in fact until a very few years ago—we all regarded England as the very model of an integrated homogeneous nation. College textbooks still repeat over and over the theme of the homogeneity of the English people, explaining in that way England's ability to maintain her sophisticated political order. But today even England seems to be breaking into ethnic groups. The Scottish nationalist movement is growing every day. The Welsh nationalist movement is becoming more and more strident. Various parts of English culture that were thought to be indissolubly homogeneous are beginning to split apart.

In Canada, the French nationalist movement is gathering steam and insistence. Yugoslavia is composed of at least three distinct "nations," and their union is very, very tenuous. Revolts by ethnic minorities are underway in many parts of Africa; the Biafran revolt against Nigeria is the most prominent current example of this but we can expect many more to occur in the coming decades, for that unfortunate continent seems destined to go through a long, long period of struggle in which the nation-states left over from the colonial period are broken up and alternative forms of political order are developed. Events inside China are clouded in obscurity, but one aspect of the contemporary crisis seems to feature a struggle for autonomy on the part of several of the sub-states comprising that vast country. So, contrary to our usual assumption, there is considerable evidence that even as we look at it, marveling over its unparalleled power, the nation-state is being exploded from within while at the same time forces are also gathering from without to render it more and more obsolete.

In times of rapid—revolutionary—transition strange things also happen in the breasts of individuals. Most of us have inside ourselves a kind of gyroscopic guidance system that helps us thread our way in relative serenity from yesterday to tomorrow. And for the average person, I suppose, that internal gyroscope is a conservative one; that is, he would like tomorrow to be as much like yesterday as possible. Indeed all of us are "conservatives" in one sense. We make our contracts; we make our career arrangements; we plan for our families; in short, nearly everything we do is based on the assumption that society itself will proceed under the control of a reliable, conservative built-in gyroscope— one that is, figuratively speaking, a collective version of the conservative gyroscope in our own psyche.

But we also know, of course, that one of the characteristics of a society undergoing rapid transition is that its conservative gyroscope gets thrown out of kilter from time to time and no longer works well in providing the stability and predictability our individual internal gyroscopes seem to demand—or at least seem most comfortable with. So, as we go about our affairs in times of rapid transition, trying to arrange for tomorrow according to the expectations we acquired yesterday, preparing for the future on some kind of stable basis, we keep running into things that block and frustrate these expectations. Things just don't work out the way our conservative gyroscope wants them to, and our efforts to arrange the future on the pattern of the past have been forestalled at a number of points. When we run into a block that prevents our affairs from proceeding in the way we had hoped and expected, what do we do?

The normal reaction is to regard each frustrating block with extreme dislike. That is, generally speaking, such frustrations of our expectations produce hatred, and this is merely another way of talking about violence. Moreover, the same process holds in reverse for those who have radical gyroscopes inside themselves; those who feel in tune with change and are trying to advance the leading edge of the revolution. The radical may feel gratified by some of the changes taking place, but he is more intensely aware of numerous ways in which his efforts at change are frustrated, or harshly put down. Thus, the revolutionary also runs into blocks that frustrate the realization of his expectations; blocks that often assume the form of human beings, officials of one sort or another, who represent or sympathize with the Establishment. Radicals hate their blocks just as conservatives do their own. The result is, then, that times of rapid transition are characteristically times that produce, out of the normal reactions of normal people, an extremely heightened incidence of violence.

From a political standpoint, this usually results in an extremely interesting but also a very hazardous condition, which can be called a "conservative crisis." This refers, not to a crisis *in* conservatism, but rather a crisis that *produces* conservatism. This happens because one of the characteristics of a revolutionary period is that the evils that arise —let's say the problem of the civil rights revolution or of the student rebellions—cannot any longer be resolved by the traditional reformative measures that were previously effective for resolving such crises. Our student rebellion is an example. Students have always been in some form of rebellion; they've always "had it in for" the administration; they've always complained about stodgy professors and they've always hated their routine course work. Many such waves of protest have arisen throughout the past. One of the most interesting of these occurred in the late 19th Century in the movement to establish the Greek letter fraternities—now the bastions of student conservatism but initially hotbeds of revolt. The typical reaction of college authorities has been to appoint a faculty-student committee that would look into matters, produce some minor reforms, and that usually took care of the situation. But the condition of our universities today is such that to apply this type of traditional reform measure to the developing protest not only no longer resolves the conflict, but on the contrary, aggravates it. Thus, an additional characteristic of revolutionary times is that the methods of reform that previously alleviated crisis conditions instead worsen the very conditions toward which they are directed.

From a political standpoint, this brings about a curious result. Those of us who are accustomed to thinking of ourselves as liberals would normally think of voting for reform candidates whenever things get in a bad way. Usually this suffices. But what happens when we elect a reform candidate in a time of radical change? We put a man like Edmund G. Brown into the governor's office. But this puts a reformer into conditions—remembering the crisis described above—in which no reformative measures can succeed. Moreover, after all his reformative efforts have been tried, things are made worse than when he started. The reformer does not "try" to lose; rather, there is no way mere reform can really deal with the evils that come to light. So what happens? It is characteristically the reformer—the liberal—who is in office and who is blamed for the worsening of the crisis. The people react to his "failure" by replacing him with a conservative. Thus, a revolutionary situation tends to discredit liberal reformers, producing a conservative crisis that tends to favor the accession of conservatives to office. And of course, when conservatives come to power they ultimately aggravate the situation even more gravely than did their liberal predecessors.

The ghetto riots, in one sense, are anti-imperialist, guerrilla movements, like those appearing throughout the Third World. That is, our ghetto riots are being waged against a kind of despotism inside our own culture that is similar to the imperialist despotism carried out by the rich nations against the poor. Secondly, as we saw earlier, there exists in the ghettos what we call the "culture of poverty." Poverty produces a characteristic form of cultural deprivation that divides society into two classes—almost two castes—making it virtually impossible for those who inhabit the culture of poverty to rise above the conditions of their birth. On the average, the child who is born in the ghetto is going to spend his days grubbing for a bare subsistence in the same conditions of poverty that attended his birth, and will end his life little or no better off than were his parents. This means that the ghettos are, in one sense, a prison—a cultural prison. Their bleak cultural walls have something like the same effect on ghetto inmates that actual prison walls have on their inmates. For this reason, it is possible to speak of the ghetto riots as being essentially prison revolts. Indeed, anyone who remembers the television interviews with rioters after the explosion in Watts will recall that the kinds of phrases they used to describe what they had done and the kinds of complaints that they made were strikingly reminiscent of what prison rioters say when they call in reporters and try to force the warden to improve prison conditions. Moreover, prison rioters, like ghetto rioters, typically give vent to their frustrations by tearing up their own habitats. In other words, just as in a prison riot, the prisoners in our ghettos direct their violence against things in their own community—their own prison.

That is one of the reasons we say that the riots we are witnessing today are not race riots at all. They are not against whites as such; they are against the system of oppression. They are, to use a phrase that is coming into some currency, antisystemic riots; they are rebellions against the entire order of life as they know it. In that sense they are truly revolutionary movements.

What about the future? Can we expect more and more of the same, only bloodier and bloodier? Where will it all end? Black leaders are all too eager to respond to such questions, painting ever-more-distressing pictures of the future, sometimes as a come-on pitch for selling their own special brand of riot insurance—and this is an area in which we are far from being "insurance poor." It behooves us to be in the market for whatever riot insurance we can get. Some people buy guns. Some contribute to the Southern Christian Leadership Conference. For the fact is that we are all convinced the conditions of the ghettos will not be measurably improved and that the riots are going to continue —on and on. And yet, there are reasons for believing that we may not have very many more huge riots like those of Watts and Detroit. This is not a prediction. In the realm of violence, prediction is impossible. But examining the evidence helps us observe a few new developments, and their significance will remain whether or not more large-scale riots do in fact occur.

Recently I spent some time investigating conditions in the South because of a concern about whether or not the riots will move to places like Atlanta, New Orleans, Birmingham and Dallas—the big cities of the Deep South. These must be distinguished from the border cities (e.g., Cincinnati, Louisville, Washington, D. C., Baltimore), which are something else again; they exhibit very grave touch-and-go situations. But with regard to the Southern cities conditions are very different. In the first place, until recent times there were few true Northern-type ghettos in the bigger Southern cities. The reason derives from slavery and reconstruction times. Southern cities had their own peculiar form of development, which evolved in relationship to their "peculiar institution." The primary role of the emancipated Negro was as a menial servant or laborer. Slaves had been quartered on their owner's property and freed Negroes continued, often in the same quarters, to reside close to their work. The Southern cities had their grand avenues, studded with elegant mansions, but hidden between them, along the back alleys or in adjacent enclaves, were the Negro quarters. Of course, things have changed rapidly, especially since World War II, and now there is more of a concentration taking place. But even so, and even though conditions in the Negro quarters of the South may be much worse than those in Watts, the pattern typical of the Northern ghetto has not been typical of the Southern city. This means there is not the same ecological factor—the ghetto as a cultural prison—in the Southern metropolis.

A second factor may be even more important. The Southern Negro has at least some rudiments of an established subculture, in the sociological, rather than in the aesthetic sense. There is some autonomy to their subculture, and there are the rudiments of a hierarchical black class structure. The middle class is not big enough to support what sociologists define as a truly viable subculture, but it is growing, and a small upper class is also beginning to appear. The contrary has been true of the Northern ghetto. In Watts, for example, there was neither an autonomous subculture nor a hierarchical class structure in the pre-riot ghetto. Indeed, one of the most interesting things about the Northern riots is that they have led to the emergence of a nascent class structure. From a sociological standpoint, this is at least one hopeful sign. In the past, the leadership structure in the Northern Negro community was determined, not by one's role in that community but by one's relation to the external white community. Again the analogy to the prison recurs. The significance of this is that the Southern cities have Negro quarters with unbelievably miserable living conditions; but they are not, ironically enough, prison ghettos in the Northern sense.

This leads to the next basis for concluding that huge riots may not break out again. Riots are in a way like lightning: they don't strike twice in the same place. The explanation of this is that there is a strange alchemy that takes place in the ghetto as a result of, and as an aftermath of, a riot. One may understand this quickly by reading the very fine book by Eldrige Cleaver, *Soul on Ice*. Cleaver, a Black Panther, was jailed after a shoot-out with Oakland policemen. One short two-page section of *Soul on Ice* is entitled "Watts." There Cleaver makes the point that prior to the riot, to live in Watts was to bear an indelible mark of inferiority. It was a hell-hole, a prison. No Negro could claim with pride that he came from Watts. The stigma of deprivation and degradation Negroes associated with the place had connotations of "hick" or "hayseed"—the actual word for a person from Watts was "lamey." But a "lamey" is so much worse than a "hick." It means that he is a cripple—injured; he's so badly maimed there's no chance. So that's what it was to be from Watts. But what has happened since? The riot changed everything overnight. The day after the riot started, "everybody" came from Watts! People who had never even been there were saying, "Man, see what my soul brothers are doing. Now *that*'s where I come from. The brothers are really doing it in Watts." Everyone, overnight, became proud of Watts. People hundreds of miles away vicariously shared in that pride and developed simultaneously a new sense of ethnic pride.

Beyond this, there is another feature to this alchemy that is produced by riots. An illustration is provided by a story that comes from my days as a graduate student. I think it may reveal something fairly common in human experience. The post-World War II generation of graduate students were often newly married and having their first children. Probably the newborn child affects the mother and father in different ways: her love-response quite possibly is immediate and automatic; when the father first sees the newborn child, it is very much a stranger. Love is not something that is immediately and automatically associated with the newborn infant by the father. Moreover, these post-war graduate students had to work very hard, studying and writing late into every night. Often they got very little sleep. So, often when a new baby awakened and needed a diaper change, it was the harassed father who staggered to the crib to care for the crying baby. I remember vividly being told about one such night by a fellow student. Awakened abruptly by the baby's cry, his first reaction was fury. He went to the crib, grabbed the baby, roughly putting him on the bathinette. Unfastening the soiled diaper, he jerked it from under the baby who naturally cried all the more. The clean one was put in place no more gently. Then, reaching for a safety pin, anger mounting with every brusque move, he pulled two diaper corners together, inserted the pin point—and then just jabbed the baby! Not deep, you understand, but nonetheless a good healthy deliberate prick. Well, the baby let out a scream that pierced directly to the core of the father's soul. The effect of the act was profound. Before then, true love of his child had been absent. Afterward, and from that moment on, he was *hooked*. By his own violence he had transformed alienation into love.

Something like this is involved in a ghetto riot. The mere act of engaging in destructive acts against the buildings of one's own community transforms them and changes them from sources of alienation into cherished possessions. By burning a ghetto one asserts one's "possession" of it. And after anyone gets true possession of a thing, it is transformed into something new to him and he's not going to destroy it. What happens in places like Watts and Detroit when the ghetto reacts against itself and smashes down buildings and tears up streets is that psychologically, in a strange way and for the first time, they make them their own possessions. They become *hooked* on their own ghettos by their own acts of violence against them. The very rioters are the ones who end up "owning" and indeed loving the same ghetto that the night before had been a prison of alienation to them. This sentiment can be found today throughout Watts.

There are not very many Northern cities left that have not had riots. The odds seem pretty high that those will experience some kind of rioting. However, there is another factor that should be borne in mind. The riots of the future *can* be more or less abbreviated or vicarious forms of violence. In the history of revolutions it has not always been necessary for every country to go through exactly the same revolutionary stages that were first experienced by the "mother" revolution. After a revolution was pulled off in one big dramatic historically spectacular episode, its results and its effects could sometimes be achieved in other places more or less nonviolently—not entirely nonviolently, but less so than in the original home of the revolution. The violence of future riots may take a somewhat more vicarious form than in the past. Finally, the blacks themselves are becoming daily more fearful that a riot might trigger the whites into taking the "final solution." Blacks know that it is the whites, rather than themselves, who are mostly responsible for the boom market in guns and ammunition. The black community simply doesn't have that much money. They have sensed the truth in Paul Jacobs' charge that demonstrations have seen law enforcement officers lose themselves in orgies of violence that can only be called "police riots." All blacks are familiar with the box scores of Watts, Newark and Detroit, where *they* were the ones killed. However, there is one form of violence that may increase. This is terrorism: black activists may try to carry on their struggle through planned clandestine attacks on the Establishment and its representatives. This also may occur in our Mexican-American slums.

All this brings us to the question of the growing black separatist movement. It takes many many forms, but one current form is the suggestion that several Southern states be given over to Negroes to institute a separate (but equal) political order within the country. Regardless of the merits of this proposal, we should all be in favor of the *debate* about black separatism. It should not be stifled for one very important reason related to the so-called break in communications between blacks and whites since the beginning of the riots. Actually, communications have not been *newly* broken, for that implies that there was once honest and legitimate communication between whites and blacks—and this is not the case. Whites may have *thought* communication existed, but blacks knew it was not so. Today the whites are paying for not having permitted a true discussion to take place. So at every interracial meeting, whites must simply sit there and take their berating over and over and over again. In every such confrontation between whites and blacks today, the white is on trial every second—a special kind of trial by torture. The black does everything possible to irritate the white so far that finally he will slip and reveal what the black already knows is in him: namely, that lurking somewhere, no matter how liberal the white comes on, no matter how radical, lurking somewhere in him is a feeling that the black man is inferior. And the black believes that if he eggs on the white long enough, prejudice will be revealed in some way. Then the black will have proved his case and the berating can stop. That is what passes for dialogue between blacks and whites today.

Obviously, this is no way to carry on a discussion. But there is *one topic*—and to my knowledge one topic only—on which it *is* possible for whites and blacks to carry on an honest dialogue: the issue of black separatism. Blacks really want to talk about it. They want to have its implications explored. They want to have every possible kind of dialectical exchange about it. We cannot afford to sacrifice the only thing we have to talk to each other about. That's the importance of the issue of black separatism. Even whites who now believe the substantive merit of the idea to be nil must give it honest consideration.

There is one curious irony about the issue. The proponents of black separatism are Northern rather than Southern activists. But the territory coveted by these Northerners is the Southern "homeland." They envisage a mass exodus of blacks from North to South, led by themselves. Ignore, for the moment, the practical difficulties. Picture the exodus—ghetto blacks led by their activists, starting out in streams from Chicago, Detroit and Newark. The streams gather, thicken and converge on the target states. But on arrival, what do they find? A smiling, but officious welcoming committee of the indigenous black Southern Establishment. For the local black elite is not about to bow down abjectly, Uncle Tom-like, and yield position and power to the Northern refugees. On the contrary, those of the North who would have made it all possible would, on arriving at the borders of the new black republic of the South, find themselves, like all immigrants, reduced to second-class status. The Northern black activists would have to fit, as best they could, into the leftover jobs and the dismal barrios of their new republic.

People often say that there is a strange relationship in love that also is partly the opposite of love. There is a theological version of this, and it resembles Milton's proposition that God needs the Devil to show Him off. (John Stuart Mill later said that truth needs error to show it off.) There is a sense in which one cannot imagine truth without the concept of error. Some psychologists would say that it is not possible to imagine love without hate. In the hate relationship now existing between whites and blacks—and it is a violent, almost shriveling hate that comes on full blast—there is an almost equally strong love that is being suppressed. The love is more difficult to bring out at this particular moment, but it is certainly there. It is revealed indirectly by the commonly acknowledged fact that the Negro revolution is a "revolution of rising expectations": that is, it is a struggle to enjoy the full benefits of life in white middle-class American society.

Based on what I have learned through my interviews, I would suggest that thoughtful Americans can come to some far-reaching conclusions about the revolution now in process. As a frequent accompaniment to the national liberation movements of recent history, historians and sociologists have observed a deeply-felt urge on the part of the people and their leaders to "strengthen themselves." Self-strengthening means rejecting the outside world while one is weak and feeble in order to develop on one's own the resources necessary to force one's acceptance by the world as an equal. This is what black separatism really means today. The black like the white, truly and deeply wants ultimately to live in a genuinely integrated society. But he has a wisdom deeper than that of the white liberal. He knows it cannot come now, either as the white man's gift or as the black man's prerogative. He knows he must make his own future for himself in his own way so that when the proper time comes he can opt for or against integration; take it or reject it on its own merits, bearing in mind that white society, at that time, may not seem all that attractive. This is the inner meaning of self-strengthening. It is the only legitimate way to ultimate integration. The first necessity for the black man is to develop pride in himself on his own; his own sense of dignity; his own sense of having an inviolable personality; all of the things that are necessary for this will have to be done by the black for himself. There is nothing anybody from the outside can do except refrain from hampering it. For them to get actively involved would reduce the Negro to the status of protégé, merely perpetuating the traditional subordination system. What is required, ultimately, is a new social contract between whites and blacks; and a true contract can be made only between equals.

Moreover, the riots have actually furthered this aim, for one of the most important functions of the riots has been to permit Negroes to turn violence outward. Violence allowed them to sublimate the self-destructive, internalized aggression patterns of the post-Civil War period. It has provided a way for them to build their own self-respect. It has also given them avenues to power—"riot power" as an American way of life. So rioting plays the opposite role for Negroes engaging in it from what it does for whites threatened by it. To blacks, violence seems creative, constructive and power-enhancing. This does not mean that it is "good." To paraphrase William James, what the Negro (and the society in general) needs is the moral equivalent of riots: self-strengthening institutions that are officially sanctioned; *not* institutions *given* the Negro by white liberals, who complain today of being excluded from "The Movement." Today, the white liberal is one of the Negro's most serious obstacles to self-strengthening. For in wanting to help, and to participate, and be a part of The Movement, the white liberal stands directly in the way of the self-strengthening the Negro must accomplish by himself—just as he started his riots by himself. The liberal becomes, unwittingly, the *most* patronizing and the most dangerous Uncle Tom-creator confronting the Negro today. So, what *can* be done? In the first place, as we said, the solutions must be as profound as the causes. This means for one thing that we must have the faith to be innovative in spite of seeming danger. Some proposals:

The first thing is to facilitate the establishment of Negro community corporations. We must facilitate the creation and development of Black Power by providing the funds that will enable Negroes to organize their communities for themselves. Milton Kotler has actually started a few such community corporations and the prospect for their spread is quite promising.

We are facing the analogue of the problem facing the developing world. And just as the developing world insists upon developing itself, expelling its former white masters and organizing and administering its affairs for itself, so also do our Negro communities. To facilitate this we can provide them with funds for sending representatives abroad to the most successful parts of the developing world where they can learn directly about the problems of cultural development. This means funding study programs for American Negroes in Tanzania, Ghana, Israel and even Cuba. The lessons learned can be applied not only to the problems of urban organization, but also perhaps using the Israeli kibbutz model, to the problems of agricultural development throughout the South. There is no reason why the government cannot send cadres of Negroes to learn kibbutz management in Israel and then finance the acquisition of large tracts of Southern farmland where such cadres can develop creative, productive and healthful farming communities. Beyond this, there is every reason for subsidizing foreign theological study for Black Muslims in the religious centers of the Middle and Far East. But the Black Muslims must choose and administer such programs for themselves. The experience of Malcolm X in Africa was a salutary one (he returned with a change of heart about the merits of integration), and it is tempting to hope that all such subsidized students would return integrationist-minded. But the merest hint of such an intent on the part of the government would kill the program. Integration, of a new sort, will come one day, but only after the self-strengthening process has been fulfilled.

Finally, programs for the autonomous development of Negro culture must be subsidized. One might compare this to the problem of providing cultural autonomy for previously suppressed nonwestern cultures. It is, in a way, the problem facing most of the nations of the world today: there are three "nations" in Yugoslavia, and the government facilitates the development of their cultural autonomy; the same is true of Czechoslovakia. In the near future the entire world is destined to produce increasing cultural articulation for national minorities. The Negro, like the French Canadian, is fully justified in insisting on having his own autonomy.

Direct action—the sort that now issues in violence too often—must be given fuller Constitutional protection. We must have a new Constitutional right to civil disobedience. It will involve reinterpretation of the First Amendment. It will require expanding the freedom of speech clause and the clause protecting the right to petition for redress of grievances. Long ago union picketing was established as a right under the free speech clause of the First Amendment. Such actions as the Memphis garbage workers' strike that Martin Luther King espoused before his death, and even the draft resistance protest mounted by Dr. Spock and others may lead the way to the moral equivalent for riots that whites and Negroes alike so desperately need.

To reverse the effects of cultural deprivation, we must facilitate the acquisition of a specially designed and consciously engendered supplementary culture. It must be provided to all who need it virtually from birth, so that the cultural deprivation of the ghetto can be overstepped and each child can be provided with a sufficiently supportive environment that will enable him to spring to the highest possible cultural and intellectual attainments. This will require drastic programs:

One innovation is the idea of cottage schools. Blackboard jungles must be torn down and cottage boarding schools established in their place. Class sizes must be held down to something around 20. Moreover, it must be possible for the culturally deprived child to live in a good boarding school, staying with his own class through graduation. If this sounds expensive, well, it is. It is like guaranteeing a New England private boarding-school education to every child. And this is exactly what we must do.

Another prospect is multi-media homes. This may provide the ultimate solution for us all. Consider the technological possibilities we now possess. We have television, audio tapes, records, newspapers, magazines, encyclopedias, movie films and computers to run them all. We have the possibility of integrating all these into a home-sized multi-media installation. This means that we can all "subscribe" to a total information, cultural, educational and amusement "program," the way we now subscribe to separate newspapers and journals. Moreover, these programs can be specially designed for individual family needs so that we can start with the most depressed family imaginable and design a long-term multi-media cultural program in much the way insurance consultants now design lifetime protection policies for their clients. Through such means it is technologically possible to bring even the most deprived person through all the stages of cultural development, up to the highest level imaginable, within a single lifetime. To repeat, today it is possible for every person alive to move, within a decade or two, from functional illiteracy to the status of a philosopher or a scientist. The insidious despotism of the "track" system can be prevented before it gets started.

We all know that megalopolis is not only obsolete, it is the breeding ground of cultural and physical disease. We also know that it is now technologically feasible to have any kind of city we wish. Today, in Wisconsin, there is an exciting new project for the construction of an autonomous urban community of not over 250,000 people. The computer and other new technological advances now make such cultural and economic autonomy possible. But first, major changes will have to occur in the way we run our society. This brings us to our final issue: that of violence in the present student uprisings.

Although we hear much about the "generation gap" it is doubtful that any such gap really exists. Consider, for example, that a septuagenarian, Herbert Marcuse, is hailed as the prophet of the youth rebellion throughout the world. This suggests that what we call the generation gap may be really the revolutionary gap. Our young adults are already living in a revolutionary new society that most of the rest of us do not comprehend. It is the difference between their new world and the outworn world cherished by the others that makes up what they mistakenly call the generation gap. When today's elders are gone and today's youth have grown up, it is unlikely that a new generation gap will appear between them and their young. Yet, even when today's youth is middle-aged, the present gap between them and their few remaining elders will probably still exist.

It is very difficult to say exactly what the aims of the German students are, what the aims of the French students are or indeed what the aims of the Berkeley and Columbia students were and are. Some of them speak of a new "educational dictatorship" that they expect to take the place Lenin had described for the "dictatorship of the proletariat." But this is about as far as the ideology of the student rebels goes at the present. However, we do know that there are certain kinds of enemies—certain kinds of institutions—that all the students are against. They're anti-Establishment. This sentiment is present throughout the world revolution today. On the university level, this means being anti-university. Next, they're all anti-war—anti-Vietnam—everywhere, and that means they are all anti-American.

Beyond this, a curious thing has happened to the image among those who in this country we call the politicians. There has begun to appear in Germany and in France a group of the best, the brightest and the oldest of the student leaders who look forward to an entire lifetime career spent in protest politics. Not only that, there are institutions that have grown up around the leading intellectual communities and around the foundations and research institutes, which support, and can support indefinitely, large numbers of student rebels. The students work as research assistants and engage in all sorts of intellectual handicraft work. The result is that the protest leaders are able to support themselves in a lifetime of revolutionary activity. They make up what is sometimes called the New Left Establishment. They look forward to an indefinite future as professional rebels, doing very much the same thing they are doing right now.

One of the interesting things about the prospect of the student protest turning into a semi-permanent movement, derives from the theme of Robert Hutchins' book, *The Learning Society*. The Learning Society is the society that will emerge after the scientific revolution has been consummated. The quest for creature comforts will give way to the quest for culture comforts. Automation, and many other features of the scientific revolution, will make it easier for all of us to have subsistence without spending the time and effort that was necessary for its acquisition in the past. This means that there will be a change in the nature of formal education as it has been known in the past. The reason for this is very simple: formal education was previously that small span of time in one's life, ending usually around age 21, during which time one went through a formal schooling process in preparation for earning a living in business or industry; that is, in earning a subsistence. Well, if subsistence itself ceases to be the primary quest of the citizen of the future, then the formal educational process that previously prepared for it will no longer make any sense at all. This, in turn, means that our entire idea of education must be completely revolutionized. Indeed, perhaps the very idea of a set period of *formal* education must itself be abandoned and supplanted by the idea of a lifetime of learning; learning in a new key, learning as the central feature of one's lifetime career, rather than as a few years spent at school. The result, according to the Hutchins thesis, would be a "Learning Society."

It is my feeling that this analysis is essentially correct. More than that, however, it is possible that today's student protest leaders are the pioneers on the frontiers of the Learning Society. They may even be developing the "curriculum," and the kinds of commitment to the educational process that will have to break out of the formal span of years that previously prepared one for a future, and spread it throughout one's lifetime. In this sense, the patterns of "violence" of the student protest may shortly disappear as "violence" and reappear instead as the curriculum of the new Learning Society. For in essence, the Learning Society will be one in which each person's primary profession is politics—the cultivation of the civic order.

We shall have to build this new, more rational and more man-sized social order sooner or later. We might as well start now. Dr. Hutchins likes to illustrate this with a story about Marshal Lyautey, the famous 19th Century French Governor-General of Morocco. One day he asked his gardener about a beautiful tree he had seen, wishing to have more of them for his own garden. "But General," said the gardener, "that tree takes 200 years to reach maturity." "In that case," he replied, "we have no time to lose. Plant them this afternoon."

We have less time to lose—and quicker and more beautiful results to expect. We must start planting the seeds of our new and more humane culture immediately.

REFLECTIONS ON VIOLENCE

VIOLENCE AND IDENTITY
by Edmund Carpenter

Edmund Carpenter is head of the anthropology department,
San Fernando Valley State College, Northridge, California.

"Sometimes," says the Western hero in *The Virginian,* "violence is the only way. Ah wish it warn't." He never draws first. But he never hesitates "to do what he has to do." He lives in a world of violence, believes in violence. But, if that violence is to hold value, it must never exceed necessity.

The point of Western movies isn't violence but a certain image of a man, a style, that expresses itself most clearly in violence. Americans became what they beheld. In real life, Gary Cooper was General George Marshall—silent, melancholy commander of the most powerful army in history, yet winner of the Nobel Peace Prize. The aging Marshall asked only that he be allowed to hang up his guns and badge and retire to his farm in Virginia, but he was repeatedly recalled to duty when law and order required his presence on some distant frontier.

The theme of restraint, coupled with unavoidable violence, is strong in American fiction and history. It was stated at Concord: "Don't fire unless fired upon. But, if they want a war, let it begin here." Americans entered wars only after being attacked; they disarmed immediately after each. Between wars they trod lightly, carrying big sticks. No people possessed such power, yet used it so little. This puzzled Europeans. To them, power had to be exercised, preferably in conquest.

People speak of "growing violence in our society." That would be hard to achieve after Hitler, Hiroshima, Vietnam. What they mean is that once-passive groups are using violence for self-identity.

William James once wrote that no more fiendish torture could be devised than when you speak, no one answers; when you wave, no one turns; but everyone simply cuts you dead. Soon, he said, there wells up within you such hostility you attack those who ignore you and, if that fails to bring recognition, you turn your hostility inward, upon yourself, in an effort to prove you really do exist.

Twenty-five years ago, Senator Bilbo, Mississippi demagogue, went on radio to refute what he regarded as Northern slanders. With him was a Negro. "Jim here," he said, "has been my servant for over thirty years. I love Jim. My family loves Jim. Jim, northern reporters been telling folks we don't treat our niggers right. I want you to tell radio folks the truth so they hear it right from you. Tell everybody."

"You mean everybody back at the house?"

"No, Jim. I mean *everybody*."

"Everybody in Mississippi?"

"No, Jim, *everybody*. Even folks up North."

"HELP!"

Help was not soon in coming. As recently as a few years ago a pet cemetery in Washington, D.C., guaranteed that pets owned by Negroes weren't accepted. It didn't take some twisted mind lying awake nights to come up with that one. If you accept racism, such details follow naturally. Deny a man his existence, you deny his dog's existence.

Violence offers immediate identity. This is especially true for "invisible" Negroes who thereby become—instantly—very visible. In 1967, when armed Black Panthers entered the California State Assembly, pandemonium occurred. Violence is a powerful force in any quest for identity. I was present when a Negro student leaned over a conference table and said to a university vice president, "You mother-f------ s.o.b." The vice president paled. It was probably his first genuine reaction to any Negro student, perhaps to any student.

Detribalizing the African slave robbed him of all identity, creating great misery of psychic alienation. Racism brainwashed him of his past, leaving him "Wandering between two worlds, one dead /The other powerless to be born." He became an invisible stranger in a strange land.

I see television as the main force that has suddenly made the "invisibles" of our society visible to themselves and to others. Television is like a mirror: you see yourself in it, perhaps for the first time. It makes explicit that which has gone unseen.

Today's "invisibles"—Negroes, students, French Canadians, youths

—demand visible membership in a society that has hitherto ignored them. They want to be seen, acknowledged. They use clothing as weaponry: the hippie dress and grooming are designed for shock effect. Or they use the torch. But basically they "want in"; they want to participate in society from the inside and they want that society to be reconstituted to allow membership for all.

The problem of living in a society, yet not participating in it, is an inhuman one. In extreme situations, it may lead to death. This was the finding of W. B. Cannon and others who concluded that the principal factor in voodoo death and other forms of public hexing was the withdrawal of all community support from the condemned man. No one would even acknowledge his existence. "Physical integrity," writes the anthropologist Claude Lévi-Strauss, "cannot withstand the dissolution of the social personality."

On a lesser level I experienced this feeling as an ethnologist. For months after I first arrived among the Eskimo I felt empty, clumsy. I never knew what to do, even where to sit or stand. I was awkward in a busy world, as helpless as a child, yet a grown man. I felt like a mental defective. There was so much distance between us, such unnatural silences. So I smiled a lot, though smiles come grudgingly to me, and helped lift or pull, do anything. These efforts were met with stares. But gradually my feelings of stupidity and clumsiness diminished, not as a consequence of learning skills so much as becoming involved with a family, with individuals. If they hadn't accepted me, I would have remained less than an outsider, less than human.

Violence and a search for identity may at times be related, though clearly each can exist independent of the other. Violence doesn't automatically disappear the moment identity is achieved. The reverse may occur: violence may be basic to a particular identity. There are examples of tightly-knit societies, where every member is woven into the fabric of responsibility and privilege from birth to death, yet where violence is highly valued. Nor are art and other commendable enterprises simple alternatives to violence. The Aztecs devoted themselves to art and torture simultaneously. The extent of human sacrifice among them shocked even the hardened Spaniards. In one ceremony, priests sprinkled incense on a girl who personified the goddess, threw her on her back, cut off her head, caught the gushing blood in a tub, and sprinkled the blood on the wooden image of the goddess. After that they flayed the headless trunk, and one of the priests squeezed himself into the bloody skin. Then they clad him in the girl's robes, put a mitre on his head, a necklace about his neck, and feathers in his hands, and thus arrayed, they led him forth in public, all of them dancing to the tuck of the drum, while he skipped and postured at the head of the procession as briskly as he could, inconvenienced as he was by the tight and clammy skin. On another occasion, the elders of a tribe that had sent the daughter of their royal house to marry a prince arrived to find a priest dancing in her skin.

All this was done by the Aztecs, whose guardian spirits spoke to them in the twittering voice of the hummingbird, who built a glorious city off the water and who loved to arrange flowers. The contrast struck the 19th Century historian William Prescott so forcibly he suspected divergent strains in their culture. But what made him think cruelty and love of beauty are incompatible, I don't know.

VIOLENCE AND POWER
by George E. G. Catlin

George Catlin, philosopher, political scientist and author, is Vice President of the World Academy of Art and Science.

Power is the potentiality of control that can guarantee to us the conduct of our neighbors on the morrow. That control may be mutual and cooperative and, if less dramatic and revolutionary, may be more constitutional and stable in that fashion. It is a traditional German error, which still infects much academic thought, that power has to be a matter of *Macht*, of what the Latin schoolman called *dominatio*, a relationship of "over and under." Power can use force but is far from synonymous with it; and recognized power, which is authority, is the antithesis of violence. The doctrinaire antiauthoritarian, who does not recognize that authority itself provides the guarantees of liberty, who has an obsessive fixation in favor of anarchy and against power—and all politics involves the power politics of means—is blind to this. Nevertheless, it is anarchy that, recognizing no tribunal, invites the arbitrament of force and violence.

Some of the most fruitful studies lie in the border areas between disciplines. The last decade has seen immense advances in the fields of biology, ecology, anthropology, which have bearing upon the aggressive relations, not only between species, but within species, including what is ironically called *homo sapiens*. There is indeed almost universally a "pecking order"—a nonegalitarian status order; and a private or group territorial defense. But, in much of the animal world, once the ritual of assertion and defense is gone through, the ritual of coexistence, of avoidance of physical destructive attack, takes over. The walrus seeking to heave himself onto an ice-floe raps his head on the ice to acknowledge the prior sovereign rights of the walrus already on the floe. Our diplomats might be well recommended to go to school with the walrus. But, as Sir Harold Nicolson has remarked, the days of authentic diplomacy to produce peace and nonviolence are probably over, replaced by democratic or demagogic propaganda and other tribal noises primarily directed to giving euphoria to the voter-supporters back home. That these propaganda-fed supporters may be grossly ignorant of the realities is irrelevant. What matters is not these realities but either *la gloire* (which spells such baubles of sovereignty as the bomb) or the anguish of facing the draft for the boys, who want to vote on the matter. To pursue peace under conditions other than those of a fishbowl is considered undemocratic. However, it was Talleyrand and not Lloyd George who achieved a European peace that lasted for a century.

To this it may be replied that—although few people have indeed any clear view of or deep attachment to what the 18th Century would have called their "intelligent self-interest," as distinct from their emotions—one of the troubles of democracy is the apathy of the common man to other people's inconvenient interests. He has to be given a kick in the backside to wake up; and demonstrations, strikes, violence provide that kick. (Let us admit that, as recently in France, the result of the kick may be a massive reaffirmation of conservatism and the collapse of the Byronic romantics and dialogue-besotted anarchists.) It is no good preaching "democratic committeeism" to a Lenin or to a Hitler. It is precisely the Establishment, the tribunals, "the laws of war," "bourgeois international law," that they are up against. Revolution parades violence, denies consensus and distrusts alike majority votes and the so-called "reasonable man." It appeals, amid the tempest, to Caliban and to resentment and proclaims "justice," decided by itself: its arbiter is force. Thomas Aquinas approved revolution when there was no constitutional alternative; when it was guided by recognized magistrates; and, shrewdly, when it was likely to succeed. Contemporary revolutions reck little of constitutional means (too slow) or of magistrates (too conventional); but success still matters.

The human race has lasted some millions of years. With luck it has still some millions of years more in which to occupy its time and improve its stock. Yet there is an order of political priorities, chiefly based on things the human race must *not* do. It must not pollute the atmosphere or the waters; it must not despoil natural resources; it must not blow itself up. These things matter far more than the difference between communism and capitalism, or even than a purposeless education or the rush forward of production and "mad science." What this century chiefly needs is a massive sedative, a vast tranquilizer, to reduce its hysteria of anxiety and to consolidate disapproval of "means to victory" that threaten the entire existence of the race. The present refusal of cooperation by China and France invites intransigent condemnation. As Margaret Mead has shown, a stable society can connect with the limitation, not the abundance, of occasions for individual choice.

Mankind needs an authority with wisdom in deciding upon its purposes and priorities and the power to induce consensus and enforce it. Ideally it needs a world authority of unchallengeable power. As rational men we would wish an easy, voluntary consensus, following the voice of reason and of the humane, worthy and just. As rational men we also have to recognize the weakness of reason—*intellectus non movet*—the paucity of its believers, the slowness and difficulties of consensus. There will always be the fanatics and the men who for neurotic reasons cry out for political orgasm and revolutionary catharsis. As the 17th Century English statesman Lord Halifax wrote: "To govern men one must often treat them scurvily." The proposition of power is that it alone holds the final instruments of violence, in the very interest of peace. And peace, in the atomic age, is one of the few categorical imperatives of consensus. No valid claim can stand against it—certainly not those of tribalism or nationalism or the archaic one of absolute national sovereignty, complete with arms and bomb. To think otherwise is the final crime of Charles de Gaulle.

In moments of depression I sometimes think that the best thing that could happen to the world would be the restoration of the Roman Empire. The Romans, from the days of Romulus, were uncompromisingly aggressive; and, in the end, they conferred on the world the immense benefits of the *pax romana*—a desolation for their foolish enemies but a peace. Again it may well be that, within a couple of centuries, the Chinese, having "won" the biological race—a remark not in conflict with my earlier one—might dominate world policy. However, it is not the business of a political scientist to specialize in crystal-gazing about the 22nd Century.

What we can affirm is the close connection, meriting coordinated research, between social psychology and individual psychology, international violence and (as Harold D. Lasswell has insisted) personal insecurity. Moreover, the sociological evidence is abundant that personal insecurity is not by any means exclusively a matter of economic deficiency. The strain of excessive competition can stimulate violence—as can the cult of violence in "the media of information and entertainment." The need for students is for serious investment in inter-disciplinary research, under some such auspices as the Einstein-inspired, international World Academy of Art and Science, into the determinant factors of conflict, peace and war.

PROGRESS, IMPATIENCE AND ANGER
by Henry Ford II

Henry Ford, Board Chairman of Ford Motor Company, is Chairman of the National Alliance of Businessmen, which promotes the hiring of the hard-core unemployed.

The bewildering tangle of problems we face is reducible, in large part, to one problem, which can have only one answer.

That single problem is the absence of opportunity for millions of Americans. And that single answer is the creation of opportunity for every American.

The achievement of genuinely equal opportunity is, in fact, the most urgent task our nation faces. It must be placed first on the national agenda, and it must be given the massive commitment of material resources and human effort it requires.

The truth is usually more complicated than it seems, and the truth about equal opportunity is no exception. Privileged Americans believe, by and large, that substantial progress has been made against poverty, racial discrimination and urban blight. They are right, and they are understandably bewildered when they see progress greeted by impatience, anger and violence. By many measures—including income, occupation, education and political representation—progress toward equal opportunity for Negroes has been hastened markedly in recent years.

Dispossessed Americans believe, however, that equal opportunity is still a distant dream. They, too, are right and they are understandably impatient to close the gap. All the measures that show the gap is narrowing also show that it is still very wide. And the narrower the gap becomes, the more outrageous it seems that it should exist at all.

Poor Negroes are encouraged by extremists to believe that orderly progress within the structure of American life has not happened and can never happen. When this message is believed, the only alternatives that seem open are insurrection or withdrawal from white society and the establishment of a separate Negro nation within a nation. But these, of course, are not real alternatives. Insurrection can lead only to anarchy and repression. Withdrawal can lead only to continued poverty and denial of equal opportunity.

White people, too, are deceived by extremists who refuse to see the other side of the coin, who encourage them to believe that Negro unrest is the product of agitators, that equal opportunity has been achieved and, indeed, that Negroes are rapidly becoming a privileged class. When this message is believed, violence again may seem to be the appropriate response. At the very best, the fruit of such misconceptions is indifference and tokenism.

It is good that Negroes are increasingly determined to take control of their own destiny, to demand what is theirs by right and to seek the power to enforce those demands. But real black power is not violence in the streets or self-imposed segregation. Black power is the power of the purse and the vote, of knowledge and skill, of self-discipline and self-confidence. Black power is black people and white people working and voting together to elect Mayors such as Carl Stokes in Cleveland, Richard Hatcher in Gary and Kevin White in Boston. It is the kind of power that will enable Negroes to participate effectively in the revision of national priorities we must have before we can achieve victory over poverty, discrimination and slum living.

I believe that victory can be won. We have already come so far that the remaining problems are of manageable proportions. It is entirely possible to eliminate all but the most stubborn vestiges of poverty in less than a generation, if only we can summon the will and the wisdom to make the necessary effort.

VIOLENCE AND THE DECLINE OF FAITH
by Louis S. B. Leakey

Louis Leakey, British anthropologist, archeologist and paleontologist, is the author of *Olduvai Gorge, The Progress and Evolution of Man in Africa* and *Stone Age Culture of Kenya*.

Man is physiologically a mammal, although he claims to have advanced beyond the mere animal status to a psycho-social one and arrogantly calls himself *Homo sapiens*. He is probably the only member of the mammalian kingdom that regularly indulges in acts of cold-blooded killing and violence, against his own kind, within his own community. He also indulges in acts of violence and warfare against other communities of his own species, but this is somewhat different. Lions will fight other lions over the invasion of their territory or for some other reason, but they do not fight to kill, only to drive off the intruder. Many antelope males fight over territory or over possession of the females of the herd. They do so to the point of near exhaustion, but not with intention of killing. This same pattern is found throughout the mammal kingdom except in man, and in particular, so-called civilized man. Even among the primitive peoples of the world (that is to say, peoples who are primitive in respect of material culture), it is rare to find acts of violence and killing as between one man and another who belong to the same community. Acts of violence take place rather against members of other clans or tribes (e.g., head-hunting activities in Melanesia and intertribal fights in Africa). It is principally in the so-called civilized world of Europe and America that we find—tragically—the greatest tendency for man to kill or maim his fellow man under the impulse of jealousy, envy, hatred or just sheer wickedness. It clearly behooves us to seek the reasons for this departure from normal animal behavior and then work to remove the causes.

As man advanced from the purely animal stage to the psycho-social one, he developed a belief in a supreme controlling power or "god," and around this concept developed a religion. As each tribal group did so, it built up, around that belief, codes of behavior to be observed by individuals and by the community as a whole. These codes normally included rules of morality, self-discipline, self-respect, respect for others, and a responsibility to the community as a whole.

It seems to be that one of the fundamental problems besetting the civilized world today is that so many people have falsely accepted the idea that science is not compatible with any form of religious faith. They argue, therefore, that since they live in an age of science, they can and even should abandon faith. This is a wholly false concept and a wrong conclusion. A large number of the world's leading scientists believe in and have faith in a supreme power and in something more than a body of mere flesh and blood and bone for each individual; even though they may not accept any of the stylized and formal religions of the present day.

I sincerely believe that if statistics could be obtained, they would reveal that the majority of individuals who kill and commit other forms of extreme violence against their fellow men, in their own communities, are persons who have lost, or who never had, any religious faith. The underlying reasons for this loss of faith appear to me to be dual. One is the failure of many parents to help their children to understand the difference between fundamental religious faith and formal religion. The other is the failure of a majority of leaders of nearly all religious sects to differentiate clearly between the fundamentals of religious faith and the various additional dogmas and doctrines of formalized religions that have been added over the centuries.

I believe that there is another major reason why so many people living in the so-called "Western Civilization" area, and more particularly those with inadequate education, indulge in acts of violence against their fellow men. This reason is the visual impact, day after day, week after week, year after year of acts of violence shown on the cinema and television screens, and that are shown as though they were the everyday normal behavior of *Homo sapiens,* at the present time. The viewer, if he stops to think, will realize that most of what he sees is purely fictional and is being performed by actors and actresses, and that no real violence is taking place. The subconscious impact, however, is to create the impression that these acts of violence are part of normal contemporary behavior. I have had this conclusion confirmed to me by a number of conversations with poorly educated people and, particularly, those in the younger age groups.

Finally, I believe that another reason for the violence of man against his fellow man today can be found in the widespread existence of mental ill health and unbalance. This is due, in part at least, to the inability of some people to meet the challenge of the stresses of living in the modern civilized world, at a speed far beyond normal. To escape from this challenge, they fall back on mental ill health and drug taking, with very unfortunate results.

If, then, I am right in my analysis of some of the causes of so much violence today, the alternative would seem to be first, to take steps to remove the causes and, thereafter, to apply to our problems our undoubted powers of reason, and the forces of conscience. Then, with a renewal of religious faith, we will become more peaceful and more tolerant of our fellow men.

VIOLENT GOVERNMENTS, NONVIOLENT HIPPIES
by Timothy Leary

Timothy Leary, a former professor of psychology
at Harvard University, is a leading proponent of the
use of mind-expanding drugs.

The search for alternatives to violence requires, at the outset, some definitions. Frogs eat butterflies; snakes eat frogs. Self-righteous, conservative parents whip their children. Husbands beat wives. The Hiroshima bomb cremates 80,000 civilians. A man is knifed in a barroom. A boxer swings a left hook.

The life process evolving over two billion years is, in essence, a matter of rough, ruthless, lethal contact. Every form of life is at all times in dangerous contiguity—skin-membrane contact with hostile organisms. Every living creature is killing every second of its existence.

But this DNA-directed lively dance of death is certainly not the central concern of this symposium.

We admit, too, that all human beings have moments of cruelty, anger, maliciousness and psychological weaponry. But these lapses are not the central concern of this discussion.

How shall we define and specify the plague of murder that has converted this planet into a fearful and guilty nightmare?

We see all around us today a form of killing completely novel and alien to the evolutionary process. Probably quite unexpected, even shocking, to the DNA plan. A brand new form of lethal aggression that violates every morality of the genetic plan, that torments our serenity and that is the specific and only concern of this book.

What is violence?   Violence is killing by machines at a distance.

Maiming, killing, devouring other forms of life with whom you are in direct physical contact, whom you touch, with whom you struggle, whose cries and writhings and panic you see and hear and smell are the inevitables of life. Hand-to-hand fighting is an instinct built into our genes. Evolution has worked for two billion years to provide each species with muscles of offense and defense. Direct skin-to-skin killing or maiming is not violence.

Violence is long-range murder and wounding by means of machines.

Before man's maniac hands constructed the machine there was no violence.

Violence is the other side of the technological coin, the perversion of the Promethean power granted to man by an experimental divinity.

Am I violent?   Not long ago Rosemary and I moved to a hidden valley in the mountains of the Southwest—to live in one of the many hundred hippie communes that have sprung up in the remote sections of the United States. Forty young men, their wives and children dropping out of the mechanical society to live high, close to nature.

The day after our arrival Jesse Krishna drove us in a jeep up to the end of the valley where the watershed canyons down the steep slopes. As we bumped along the rough road Jesse suddenly slammed on the brakes. Rattler!

There sunning himself on the dusty switchback was a five foot diamondback. Jesse banged on the jeep door and raced the engine. The serpent rose up, looked at us and slowly glided into the bushes.

We all felt good about not killing the deadly snake, about deciding to live with him, respecting his claim to the land.

Who is violent? Man, and only man is violent.

Every other species of God's creation takes its chance in the membrane-to-membrane, eye-to-eye, fang-to-claw dance of survival.

Man is the only species who violates by distance-weaponry.

Am I violent? Sitting with Rosemary on a hill above our hippiecommune, high and happy from smoking dope, I announce that I have never deliberately used a machine to kill. Fish? Yes, I have fished. In the bay of Zijuatenejo I caught a silver, day-glow, glistening salmon and held his life throbbing in my hands and said the Unity-of-Life prayer from the Tibetan Book of the Dying and placed him in the tackle box. Am I violent?

Which human beings are violent? Most human beings are not violent. Mean? Yes. Angry? Yes. But only a small minority of human beings violate the natural plan and these men of violence are easily located. Men who construct, distribute, possess and use violence-machines, distance-weapons, firearms, are violent.

We note here that it is the human male not the female who is violent. Women can be impossibly mean. They can drive us cruelly to despair. But note this, the human female is too close to the rhythms and roots of life to use violence-machines. Does not the thought of a gal with a gun or a lady bomber-pilot give you a queer, freaky sense of rare, twisted, lesbian sexuality? Women are not violent.

Neither are men who attack me in face-to-face confrontation. Those who hit me, rush at me with sword or stick, men who wrestle me down with their own muscle power. These are aggressive but not violent. They do not violate the ancient cellular rules of the life game. They may be murderous, dangerous, but my DNA code has prepared me for two billion years to expect and deal with close contiguous assault. I am genetically guarded against this possibility. It is the distance killing that violates my animal security. Martin Luther King never saw his assassin. Neither does the napalmed Vietnamese peasant.

Which men are violent? Which men specialize in killing at a distance? You know who.

Paid, hired government agents account for 99 per cent of the violence that devastates and terrorizes this planet.

Consider violence in the United States:

(1) The American Air Force is the most violent, violating institution known to man. By conservative estimate the U.S.A.F. controls and is trained and straining to use more than 50 per cent of the violating energy available to Americans.

(2) The United States Navy with its sleek Polaris bullets is probably the next most potent source of violence. Shall we estimate the Navy controls 20 per cent of our violating capacities? Professionals in navy blue are proudly Number Two in killing.

(3) The U.S. Army and Marine Corps are a vigorous third in the violence race. What a fearful roster of distance-killing machinery the Army distributes to its millions of involuntary, drafted telescope-sight gladiators.

(4) Next on the list of violence-producers is the police constabulary of this country. The federal agents, FBI, CIA, FDA, narcotic agents, customs officials, the state police, the county sheriffs, the municipal fuzz. Each with a machine of death strapped to his side.

Totaling these four categories of self-righteous destruction, we estimate that paid government agents are responsible for 90 per cent of the machine killing and possess more than 90 per cent of the killing technology. It is interesting that in almost every country, our own included, the first function of the military and police is to employ violence or the threat of machine-violence against its own citizenry. That is, to protect the Establishment against restless and aggrieved competition.

During the last 20 years, which has seen a tremendous acceleration in the manufacture and possession of killing-machines, only a small per cent of these distance-weapons have been used in defense against equally armed foreign invasions. The dictators' jets roar off South American fields to frighten the peasants. America supplies the juntas of the world with violence-equipment to maintain the civil order. Greek, Guatemalan, South African agents crouch in city streets behind machine guns. African politicians war for civil control. Violence in defense of invasion is actually a rare event. It's more fun to kill unarmed civilians.

(5) A fifth source of violence in this country is located in the arms-bearing citizenry—Mr. Joe Jones and his home arsenal.

Now the possession of firearms by civilians is not an accidental, inexplicable, statistical phenomenon. The social characteristics of the gun-bearing civilian are quite obvious. The "kill-for-sportsmen," the gun-buffs, the armed householders tend to be the super-patriotic, the hawks, the Southerners, the Texans, the American Legionaires, the Anglo-Saxon Protestants—descendants of those who killed the Indian and fought the fraternal Civil War for economic power.

Civilians who own violence-machines are exactly those who are most identified with the government and the military establishments. Dissenters don't arm.

Any patriot loves machine-distilled alcohol. The Air Force, and the Navy and Army and the Marines, and the gun-civilians all rely on booze to support their violence.

It is also relevant to mention the trite but always awful fact that violence is profitable: that the manufacture of violence-machinery absorbs the overwhelming majority of our national budget, that the professional military, a notoriously materialistic, nonspiritual group, make a good living off violence, and that the violence-industry of this country has developed the most powerful political lobby in the capital.

(6) A sixth source of violence is robbers, criminals and gangsters. But contrary to the impression given by the Establishment's mass media (TV screens blazing with guns of the wicked Bonnie and Clyde), criminal hoodlums account for an insignificant per cent of the armed

mayhem in this country, and the world. Gangsters today are business-men who invest in armament stock issues. The petty hustlers, the armed robbers comprise less than one per cent of the violence.

(7) In the mind of the average middle-aged American, the Negro is currently seen as the greatest threat to the security of the country. This is nothing less than a paranoid delusion.

In fact, the American black man is one of the least violent people on the face of the earth. For 400 years the white man has ruthlessly elim-inated the aggressive, self-confident, black man and economically deprived him of access to violence-machinery because distance-weapons cost white money.

Black Power, the current terror, is nothing less than the discovery by certain articulate blacks that blacks and browns have not been vi-olent enough in a nation that is obsessed with violence.

Even in these days of occasional riot and looting the incidence of ma-chine-violence by blacks against whites is amazingly low. When Stokely shouts, "don't loot you a TV set, loot you a gun" he is telling his fol-lowers to become like patriotic Americans. I don't share these aspira-tions but I completely sympathize with his logic.

(8) Are the dissident youth and psychedelic young violent?

We are told by the media that the key issues in the 1968 political cam-paigns are violence in Vietnam and violent crime at home. Dissenting youth, black and white, are the vulnerable targets of the get-tough-crack-down-end-this-permissiveness program. The Nixons and Reagans and Wallaces and Daleys wish to mobilize military-police forces to deal with the protesters and the hippies.

The facts, however, will surely show that the hippies, campus pro-testers, dope-smokers, long hairs, acid heads, detached drop-outs (already the victims of discrimination and harassment) are the least vio-lent of any group in the world.

There was no gunfire in the love-ins, or at the barricades at Co-lumbia. If President Kirk had walked into his besieged office with his staff and rolled up his sleeves and said to the students drinking his sher-ry, "O.K. let's talk it out or have it out man to man," the protesters would not have used metal machines to puncture the soft body of Mr. Kirk. There was never any danger to the skins of the multi-millionaire trustees of Columbia. Nor of the Sorbonne. Nor of San Francisco State.

Remember, too, that over 50,000 young Americans have meekly been led off to jail by gun-toting policemen for violating the draft and marijuana laws. Peaceable people. Gentle crimes of conscience and personal behavior.

The politics of paranoia. The obvious truth about violence in the United States is this: it is the rulers of this country and their patriotic partisans who are totally committed to a society of violence and the first target of their violence (in this country as in other countries) is the nonviolent, pacifistic majority.

The American military-industrial establishment manufactures violence-machines, distributes them to violent men throughout the world and keeps the American populace conveniently addicted to magazine-movie-television orgies of machine-murder.

The American government is sick, fatally sick, of metal-weapon poisoning.

Am I violent? Shouts from the barn.

A group of the long-haired, bearded psychedelic brotherhood is crowding around the barn door. There, coiled, head erect and swaying, tail buzzing with electric warning, is a serpent.

Travis runs to the toolshed and returns with a pole onto which he has looped a leather thong. He pokes the loop near the rattler. All the hippies and wives and children chant "OM," (the ancient Hindu prayer of cosmic unity). The serpent slides up and puts his flat, wedge-shaped head through the noose. Travis pulls the strap and swings the snake into a canvas bag. He drives a few miles down the road and releases the serpent.

How pious we all are.

Are you violent? In politics there is an implacable Gresham's Law: the violent drive out the gentle. The wicked drive out the good. In the name of the state every emerging leader of the peaceful majority is routinely assassinated by a patriot.

Gandhi is shot by an ultra-patriotic Brahmin who thinks the Mahatma is too tolerant to the Arabs.

Malcolm X, at the moment of his conversion to Brotherhood, is gunned down by some group that is strangely protected by the government. Christ is murdered by patriotic Jews and Roman soldiers. The young, tousled-haired leader of the young, J.F.K., was killed by a man trained in sharpshooting by the U.S. Marines and loyal, in his twisted fashion, to someone's secret service. (You see it doesn't really matter which government. They are all criminally violent.) Martin Luther King is assassinated by a Southern patriot who hates reds and niggers. The young tousled-haired leader of youth, R.F.K., is gunned down by a man fanatic in his devotion to a violent Arab leader.

The violent seek power. The violent get power.

Who is violent? Governments are violent. Any patriot who supports, belongs to, identifies with a violent government is violent.

Are you violent?

The simple solution.   The violence problem is simple. If you want to get rid of violence on this planet just disarm. Just destroy all death-dealing machines.

 Each individual must disarm himself. Any author or reader of this book who possesses a machine-weapon designed to rend flesh is violent.

Each government must disarm. Totally. There is no excuse, no explanation to God or to the DNA code, that can justify the existence of one distance-killing machine on this earth.

How to deal with a violent government.   There is one easy, direct, immediate way to get your government to disarm.

Secede from the government of the violent, by the violent and for the violent.

Do what your forefathers did in times of national insanity. Drop out! Start your own country!

Every God-loving, peace-loving, nonviolent person on this planet can, in 10 minutes' time, disaffiliate himself from his unholy rulers.

Just sit down with your family and peace-loving friends and write your own Declaration of Independence. Sign it. Mail it off to the Bureau of the Census. "Subtract 12 from your list, gentlemen."

Turn in your draft card and your social security card. Inform the Internal Revenue Service about your secession. Send your passport back to the state department.*

Any political action within the framework of a violent government is at best hopeless and at worst suicidal. Do not the tragic events of 1968 make this clear? Does not the history of Naziism make this clear?

Today, as in 1936, you are either a good German or a good man.

Of course, you may get into trouble if you secede from a violent government. Right. But today, as in other historical eras, it is sadly true that if you are not in trouble with your government *you are* in trouble. Notice how beautifully this formula works regardless of the political stripe of your country. If an American or a Russian or a Greek or an Arab is not in political trouble with his government he is in real spiritual trouble.

Am I violent?   The motto of the hippie movement is: Turn-on, tune-in, drop-out.

You turn-on with sacramental drugs that create the inner condition of peaceful, reverent, harmonious euphoria.

You tune-in with acts of reverence and aesthetic prayer.

You drop-out by detaching yourself from the violent society and its computerized, impersonal, inhuman technology.

The hippies throughout the world are leaving the urban machineries and retiring to remote, secluded areas. It happened during the fall of Rome exactly the same way.

Living on the land makes for dramatic confrontations with natural forces that provide interesting revelations about the nature of violence.

Our psychedelic brotherhood buys eight horses for the ranch in the valley. The price is cheap, as is the land, because in a technologically insane society machines are expensive, life is cheap.

We have two stallions and six mares.

* *My own secession from allegiance to the United States of America was written in June 1968 and can be found in the form of a "Declaration of Evolution" to be published in my book "Politics of Ecstasy."*

The mares are placed together in one corral but the stallions are separated with the warning that they must not be in the corral of the mares or each other. But someone goofs and the two studs confront each other. Shrill, ear-breaking cries of rage. They paw the ground and rush at each other with earthshaking lunges. The great golden palomino stands on his hind feet and crashes down on his brown rival. His teeth rip the brown coat. His legs are as big as tree trunks. He whirls to the side and lashes out his back hooves in powerful kicks. We rush in to grab bridles and lead the brown stud limping and bleeding back to his own corral.

The awesome, raw, fierce energy of the animal kingdom.

Calvin is working behind the big farm house. He suddenly darts back in alarm. He came within two feet of stepping on a coiled rattler. He runs to get the noose but by the time he returns the serpent has disappeared. Four children under the age of six were playing naked within 15 feet of the deadly creature.

A powerful racial concern wells up among the parents of the gentle brotherhood. "I'll take my own chances with a rattler. I can wear boots and even if I get hit it's only a swollen leg and an unexpected acid-high. But the kids. They go barefoot. One bite and they've had it."

That night the hippie fathers, bearded and bare to the waist, sit by the fire under the statue of the Buddha and meditate. Then it is decided that rattlers around the house shall be killed. To protect the young of the species.

The next day Calvin tells me with excitement that he surprised a rattler down by the windmill and killed it with a rock. We walk down to the pasture and Calvin takes a stick and gingerly lifts up the thick, diamond-studded, limp rope of snake.

We decide to cut off the rattles and place them by the Buddha shrine.

Violence and drugs.   It may not come as a surprise that I end this essay on the hippie philosophy of nonviolence with a discussion of drugs.

Almost every person and every culture in the world uses some kind of consciousness-changing chemical. Complex and deeply-sacred rituals and taboos always surround the use of these drugs. The sacred drug focuses the spiritual activities of the culture. The daily and weekly rhythm of social life invariably pulses to the drug beat. What does an admiral, or a Boeing executive, or an enlisted man or a cop do when he hears the five o'clock bell and drops his distance-killing machine and heads home? And what does he do at the Saturday night party?

The kind of conscious-changing chemical, its preparation, its distribution and its mode of usage is invariably the diagnostic key to the soul, the essence ethic, the seed ritual of a society.

The Judeo-Christian civilization uses alcohol as its ritual sacrament. In the good old days fermented wines and beers provided the mystery, the magic, the emotional release, the altered state of awareness that men call the religious experience. But as Western culture became totally mechanical, the manufacture and distribution and use of alcohol changed disastrously along with the rest of the social society. The manufacture of wine and beer, which used to be a personal, priestly, burgomeister, vintner phenomenon, changed to the impersonal factory production of oceans of distilled spirits. Hard booze, flooding out in millions of gallons to intoxicate and stupefy the world.

The use of alcohol is no longer a ceremonial ritual but an intrinsic part of a mass production, robot civilization supported by, and now worshipping, machines of violence.

Guns and booze have become the ritual equipment of the new Western crusade.

Alcohol is a drug that specifically turns on the emotions. Leads to extremes of interpersonal display. This was most useful in the days when village and town life was dull, phlegmatic, uneventful. A roistering drunk on the Saint's day was a necessary way of emotionally loosening up a tight-knit social order.

But in the hands of an industrial, highly energized, competitive culture, obsessed and possessed by machines of violence, alcohol is tragically the wrong drug of choice.

Am I violent?   Jesse Krishna, eternal charioteer, is to drive Rosemary and me down to the desert to visit a Navaho hogan. As we drive down the road away from the hippie ranch Jesse shouts, "Rattler" and keeps the car rolling up to and over the snake. "I ran over him," he shouted. "He's still alive," said Rosemary. "We've got to get him," I shouted. I jumped out of the car, grabbed a stone and ran down the bank after the snake. I was barefoot but had no fear. "I hit him," I shouted. I was impatient with Jesse who was slow to come to my aid. Jesse half-heartedly picked up a stone and lobbed it. I was berserk with excitement. I ran down past the snake and grabbed an iron rail lying in the pasture. The snake was slithering away at top speed. I ran close to him and lifted the heavy bar and brought it crashing down. It jarred my hands. I missed. I felt as if something in me or outside had pushed my arms causing me to miss. Without hesitation I lifted it up, again and again smashing the serpent's back, aiming for his head. I was possessed by some fury and unusual strength. Jesse Krishna stood watching me with a curious look on his face. He kept saying, "Enough, enough, it's dead."

I was heaving and panting going back to the car.

We continued our trip. We ate some sacrament and by the time we reached the desert we were very high.

We were so high we got lost and didn't care and drove through the desert digging the land and the air and the colorful sunset.

Jesse Krishna was quiet. After a while he said he was still thinking about the snake. I had forgotten about it but as soon as he mentioned it, a whole new level of reality suddenly clicked into consciousness. Sudden catastrophic revelation into my blind murderous actions.

We move into the Garden of Eden with a heavenly Brotherhood. In one week I have changed from a life-affirming pacifist into a maniac who leaps out of cars and slays snakes before the disbelieving eyes of my wife and my young guru. The serpent in the garden and the sudden knowledge of good and evil bisecting the unity of our life. I sank into a psychedelic dark-night-of-the-soul. The serpent was a divine resident of the paradise. And I slew him. Irrevocably. In spite of my years of Hindu meditation I was just like the rest of them. From within me had suddenly burst forth this instinctive, blind spasm of murder. Implacable, active remnant of my genetic past. Do we all carry within us this deep ungovernable instinct to kill?

To make the world nonviolent, your best hope is dope.   In the year 1960 a small group of psychologists centered in Cambridge, Massachusetts, came to the conclusion that the key to psychological change (in any and all forms) was biochemical; that the only effective methods for altering conditioned patterns of human behavior were pharmacological.

This premise seemed to us so self-evident that we still wonder how any psychopharmacologist, neurologist or open-minded student of human psychology can disagree with these biochemical predictions.

The practical implication of this theory is that the most direct way to loosen up the neurological rigidity that has legislated violence and suffering throughout the world was *dope:* the judicious systematic, knowledgeable self-administration of consciousness-expanding drugs.

It is of interest that a skeptical, sophisticated intellectual like Arthur Koestler has recently made a similar point. Mr. Koestler seems to be saying that the conflict between the older brain and the younger associative areas of the cerebrum (both of which are necessary for survival) can only be harmonized by the correct drugs.

In 1960 our group of Cambridge psychologists initiated a deliberate plan to encourage the thoughtful self-administration of drugs which we believed could expand and unify the human mind.

We were well aware of the fact that a concerted attempt to help people become more happy and peaceable would run into immediate trouble with the violent status quo. History teaches us that anyone in the past who has been effective in stimulating his fellowman to gentleness was quickly killed or imprisoned by militant patriots. The recent ordeals of Dr. Spock, Dick Gregory, Joan Baez, Rev. Coffin demonstrate that this tradition is still with us.

Our plan to psychedelicize the world thus involved a deliberate tactic of civil disobedience.

We have never campaigned to make legal our gentle herbs and

drugs. How can a sacrament be legal, i.e., approved of by an un-Godly, violent government?

The fact that our sacraments—L.S.D., marijuana, peyote, mushrooms—were proscribed by Caesar seemed to us to be exquisitely fortuitous.

The very act of ingesting a peaceable drug became, quite automatically, a double gesture of gentle detachment—both symbolic and neurologically real.

Each one of the several million Americans who has "turned-on" illegally in the last few years has had to take some sort of internal stand against the government; has committed an act of passive, quiet defiance; has made a statement of distrust in the government. "We just don't believe you or accept your legislative meddling in our private lives."

The ingestion of an illegal psychedelic drug is much more effective than other acts of passive disobedience. Thoreau refuses to pay a tax. Gandhi collects the forbidden salt. But the tax form and the salt do not bring about neurological changes. Draft-card burnings, sit-ins, illegal demonstrations are part of the government game. You are playing on "their" chess board. Burning their cards, trespassing in their streets and buildings. The unfortunate effect of overt political acts is that your consciousness becomes entangled in the very web of control and violence that you wish to avoid.

The value of fasting and spiritually-oriented illegal drug-taking is that the act also changes your nervous system in the same direction as the symbolic meaning. The person who fasts or smokes marijuana feels less aggressive and more calm. In the words of the young, he is "stoned," he is "high."

Another advantage in illegal drugs as instruments of revolution is that their acquisition and ingestion automatically involve you in conspiracies that require mutual trust. A brotherhood of like-minded spiritual accomplices. The effects of this comradeship cannot be overestimated, especially among the young. As you get "high," as your nervous system glows with warm, tender revelation, the same thing is happening to your fellow-conspirators—who are chancing the same social risks as you.

I believe that very few middle-aged Americans (and perhaps few of the contributors to this volume) are aware of the revolutionary significance of the psychedelic drug phenomenon as a force for social change, as an instrument for nonviolent political change.

Control of economic power was the aim of the Marxian and Keynesian revolutions.

Control over your own nervous system, freedom from the machine and from machine-violence is the aim of the neurological or psychedelic revolution. And the key is the chemical.

For a peaceable, harmonious world today, your best hope is dope.

For those readers of this book who find that they are unable to secede from our violent government, for those who are unable to say "In order to become a free man I can no longer be an American"—the following prescription may be enlightening.

During the next few months try an experiment in personal disarmament. Arrange to have seven psychedelic sessions—each one carefully planned and designed to be an exploration into the sources of your own inner harmony. Arrange, if possible, to share these experiences with beloved friends who share your nonviolent aspirations. If you have trouble finding pure psychedelic sacraments, go to a member of the only authentic voice of the future, a teen-age friend. If you have one. From his high school or college he can get you the inside dope.

Perhaps this psychedelic alternative to violence may give you peaceable visions and insights into the unified future.

But if you are not ready to try this experiment in neurological disarmament, don't be concerned. Your kids are doing it for you, and through them and by them the currents of violating violence now charging the world will soon be alternated.

Am I Violent?   The day after I slew the serpent Calvin came up to me and confessed that he felt terrible about killing his snake. "Man, I can't go around this Garden of Eden hating my fellow creatures."

I told him about my self-revulsion and we agreed that the snake hunt was over.

I walked down the road and found the still body, now stinking and covered with flies. I carried it back at arm's length to our hogan and cut off the rattles for our shrine.

I said to Rosemary, "I'll bury the snake under the little maple tree by the front door and we'll call it the serpent tree and it will be a Holy reminder to us."

Rosemary said, "Put an apple in its mouth when you plant it and that will be the end of the very old bad-snake trip."

May our Fathers and our Sons-to-come protect us from violence.

end . . . . .

VIOLENCE AND THE PURPOSE OF EDUCATION
by S. Radhakrishnan

Sir Sarvepalli Radhakrishnan, former President of India, is a statesman, philosopher, educator and author.

Democracy rightly interpreted and properly implemented is the only alternative to violence. Whenever people get together there are bound to be differences that have to be adjusted by democratic processes and procedures. Differences need not give rise to discords and disorders. We are trained, however, to the politics of violence, subversion, infiltration and guerrilla warfare. In these days of nuclear development conflicts may lead to a nuclear war that will be the greatest threat to the survival of civilized values. Therefore thoughtful, informed and intelligent people are keen to avert this greatest danger to humanity.

Years ago, Woodrow Wilson said: "To fight you must be brutal and ruthless and the spirit of ruthless brutality will enter into the very fiber of our national life, infecting Congress, the country, the policeman on the beat, the man in the street."

Unfortunately the kind of education we get and the practices we adopt encourage the use of violence for the settlement of disputes. The German poet Friedrich Hölderlin said that "what has always made the state a hell on earth has been precisely that man has tried to make it a heaven." The fallacy is that my heaven cannot be yours— the Declaration of Independence fashioned the finest phrase in the English language in the protection of individual liberty: the right not to get, but to pursue one's personal aspiration and happiness. Nationalism, colonialism, racism, economic exploitation—we acquiesce in them though they are essentially undemocratic. We think our nation is superior to other nations and it is our duty to impose our ideals on others. This is the root of colonialism. Similarly we think that our race is superior to other races and so we ill-treat those who do not belong to our race. Apartheid is an illustration of our mode of thinking. It is bound to produce feelings of humiliation and resentment among those who are supposed to belong to the inferior races. Even in an affluent society like America, as many as 10 million people suffer from undernourishment, and in other countries the proportion of the poor to the rich is large.

When we exalt nationalism, colonialism, racialism and economic exploitation of the masses, which are essentially undemocratic principles, we can enforce these ideals only by a resort to violence. That is what we are doing in Viet Nam, West Asia and other parts of the world. Violence is practised largely for doing things that are essentially undemocratic. We are habituated to resort to arms whenever we cannot get our way. We invent a thousand excuses to justify our use of violence.

What is essential is the re-education of mankind. We must educate men in the true principles of democracy that is natural to human kind and not distort their vision and values. We must educate them to believe that violence is non-natural to man. It is never right to do wrong. When Gandhi was told that it would be difficult to attain freedom by nonviolent methods, he said that his country might go under and it would not hurt him. When an important journalist of Madras told him that it was necessary for him to advertise alcoholic drinks in his paper and said "I must live," Gandhi's answer was: "I don't see any necessity." When Jesus died on the cross he did not care for material survival but stood for fidelity to spiritual principles. Most of us repudiate spiritual ideals for the sake of material survival.

The only alternative to violence is a sound system of education. We should abhor the use of force to enforce our own views of national, racial or economic superiority.

We need a revolution in our modes of thinking and habits of behavior. We should produce a new type of man. A fearless, greedless, hateless human being is our aim. So long as our social order continues, exalting our own nation, race, class, we cannot produce such a type of human being. A social revolution is the only answer to violence.

Unrest is a worldwide phenomenon. People live in fear and uneasiness. Every nation finds itself torn apart by racial hatred, intolerance, misunderstanding and violence. We are living in a sick society afraid of our own future. Some 2,500 years ago the Hebrew prophet Malachi sought to end domestic discords by asking: "Have we not all one father? Hath not one God created us? Why do we deal treacherously every man against his brother?" David said even before this: "Behold how good and how pleasant *it is* for brethren to dwell together in unity!" We have to make this prayer into a living reality.

In this mechanized world man has lost his inwardness. He is full of frustrations. There is a difference between his normal beliefs and actual deeds. We have to enable him to see the contradiction in his life that makes him behave like a mad man in his so-called decent social order.

The purpose of education is to help us to fight against evil things and create a more perfect society. Social progress cannot be achieved by external means. It is determined by man's intimate transcendent experiences. We must work for the renewal of heart, the transformation of values. We must work for a community that is wider and deeper than the State.

The great spiritual leaders are the guardians of the values of the society. They help to develop friendship and fellow feeling among the peoples of the world. They refuse to look upon anything smaller than humanity as the object of their love. It is for these leaders to serve society with integrity. They must create a social consciousness and a sense of responsibility that transcend the limits of a political community. They see unity in the midst of diversity and make others see it. There is a spirit in man that delights to do good and no evil, to endure all things, not to revenge any wrong, real or imaginary. In this centenary year of Gandhi's birth we must remember his message: "Outlive all anger and wear out all cruelty." He rejoiced in suffering for this insane world.

THE SPIRIT OF VIOLENCE AND THE MATTER OF PEACE
by Alan W. Watts

Alan Watts, former Anglican priest, is a philosopher, author and leading U.S. exponent of Zen Buddhism.

The idea that man has an instinct for violence must be questioned. Instincts, whether for violence, survival, reproduction or food, would seem to be causes or explanations of the same type as humors, demons or "acts of God"—that is to say, mythical agents or starters for processes that we do not fully understand, like the mysterious "it" in "it is raining." It is of great interest that many behavioral scientists now prefer to speak of *drives* rather than instincts, implying that when people feel angry, hungry, or lusty they feel like passive puppets, driven by forces beyond themselves. But this implies that "myself" is something less than my whole body and all its processes—a notion that I find absurd, however much it may correspond to our normal, but socially conditioned, ways of thinking and feeling.

Almost all civilized peoples have been brought up to think of themselves as ghosts in machines, as Arthur Koestler put it: as souls or spirits in alien bodies, as skin-encapsulated egos, or as psychic chauffeurs in mechanical vehicles of flesh and bone. We have learned to identify ourselves exclusively with a part-function of the brain, a sort of radar or scanning function that is the apparent center of conscious attention and voluntary action. Although this center feels responsible for deliberate thinking, walking, talking and handling, it knows next to nothing of *how* it manages to accomplish these actions. Furthermore, it experiences all the so-called involuntary functions of the body as events that simply happen to it. Thus it feels driven and passive with respect to strong emotions, to the circulation of the blood, and to the secretion of adrenalin.

However, there are those who feel that this separation of ego from body is the distinctively human achievement. It enables us, within certain limits, to subject nature to reason and to control what "merely happens" by the disciplines of art and science. It enables us to stand aside from ourselves and be critical of our own behavior, in short, to be self-conscious. Above all, it is supposed to be that unique function that "raises us above the animals," a boast that is beginning to sound increasingly hollow, since no mere animal seems to be preparing to destroy the planet as a by-product of war against its own species.

My home is at present a large boat in a quiet harbor where we are surrounded by birds—wild duck, grebes, pelicans, terns and gulls galore—and the latter are so ravenously hungry that they sometimes appear to me as winged tubes with internal organs like a vacuum-cleaner. Why do I feel that this world of birds is in some way more sane than the world of people? It must be hard work to be a bird, having to process enormous quantities of food through those short intestines. From the way in which gulls scramble and jostle each other for bits of bread, you would imagine that a single gull would be most happy to eat alone. But if you throw a crust to a lonely gull, it calls in a way that brings every other gull within hearing to the spot. Perhaps it doesn't know how to calculate, or just doesn't know how to restrain its squawks of delight. Maybe it isn't really an individual, but simply the subordinate organ of a gull-group (something like a communist). Men have an envy of animals so deep that they will use any and every reason (the contradictions be damned) for proving their inferiority.

The root of this envy is the belief that animals, and especially free-flying birds, have no sense of responsibility. They hunt, nest and breed without calculation, just as we breathe, hear and grow hair. They "take no thought for the morrow," whereas self-conscious and self-critical man, with his sense of being in at least partial control of his actions, lies awake at night trying to make up his mind about important decisions or chiding himself for past mistakes. The individual human being is perpetually at odds with himself for not being sufficiently thoughtful, decisive and self-controlled, regarding himself as civilized to the degree in which he manages to press this inner conflict to victory for the rational ego. Civilization is therefore attained through man's violence against himself—reflected in the flogging of his children, dogs and horses and in the brutal or subtle tortures inflicted upon those less successful and cunning groups of bandits known as criminals. More and more, the scientists are saying that man must now take his future evolution into his own (i.e., the ego's) hands and rely no longer upon the caprices of "natural selection." Yet those who speak thus do not seem to realize that this is going to require increasing violence against "deviant" forces within the individual and within society. The aspiration to direct evolution is also the aspiration to be "as God," and thus—as God is generally conceived in the West—to be dictator of the world.

But, as the psalm says, "Behold, he that keepeth Israel shall neither slumber nor sleep." This is really the same as the saying that "there is no peace for the wicked," for those who, like the tyrant-image of God, take the law into their own hands. For our traditional model of the universe is basically military.

> *God, the all-terrible King,*
> *Who ordainest*

Great winds Thy clarion
And lightnings Thy sword.

The imperious violence of intelligent spirit against intractable and mindless matter is man's projection upon the universe of his own internal split, which is what keeps him awake at night worrying about his decisions—along with "he that keepeth Israel."

The basic problem is, of course, that law and reason are linear systems expressed in verbal, mathematical or other forms of notation, of symbols strung out in a line to represent "bits" of information selected by the narrow spotlight of conscious attention. The physical world, by contrast, is at any moment a manifestation of innumerable and simultaneous energy-patterns that, when we try to translate them into our clumsy linear symbols, seem impossibly complex. Actually, the world is not complex. Complexity is in the task of trying to figure it out with words or numbers, which is like trying to keep count of all the leaves in a constantly changing forest, or measuring the Atlantic with a hypodermic needle.

Nature can be "figured out" up to a certain indeterminate point, if we proceed patiently and humbly. But if at any time we decide that we actually know "the Truth," what the law of nature is, and therefore what is the right course of action, we shall find ourselves in the paradoxical situation of having to compel nature to submit to what we conceive to be its own laws! As we say, "Dammit, why can't you be natural!" In other words, it is only by violence that the actual course of human and other physical events can be made to fit the oversimplified patterns in terms of which we attempt to describe it. We are like Procrustes, the mythical Greek who stretched or amputated visitors to fit his guest-room bed.

We are working, then, on the often tacit assumption that the rational ego is a stranger and invader in the physical world, representing a conceptual and ideational order in necessary conflict with the chaotic complexity of nature. But when this supernaturalist assumption is brought out into the open it is hardly credible since we also believe, at least in theory, that consciousness and intelligence arise through spontaneous evolution and are manifested through neural organizations that, as yet, we hardly understand.

This may be a "leap of faith," but I feel that if I am to trust myself I must bet on my entire nervous system (and the environment that, inseparably, goes with it) as distinct from a logic of words and numbers considered as something superior to its own neural matrix. For my brain is immeasurably more omniscient than my mind: it coordinates simultaneously more variables, more rhythms and patterns of bodily behavior, than I (as ego) could possibly comprehend in a hundred years of study. But I can see no sense in restricting the definition of "myself" to the process of conscious attention, volition, and symbolization. I must admit my whole body to the definition of "myself" and so, in a certain way, assume responsibility for all that it is and does. After all, if I do not trust the matrix of my conscious intelligence I have no assurance that this very mistrust is either well founded or well informed.

When they contemplate their own bodies Westerners are apt to feel, with the psalmist, that they are "fearfully and wonderfully made"— that some agency and intelligence quite apart from themselves manufactured this intricate machine, which, in the same breath, they will "put down" as natural chaos or merely animal functioning. Thus to identify oneself with one's whole body is seen, ambivalently, as both blasphemy and as surrender to the blind forces of the Unconscious. Whatever our metaphysics, we insist that inner conflict between ego and body, reason and instinct, is the essential condition of civilized life. But this attitude is penny-wise and pound-foolish, for when we look at the trend of civilization as a whole we see a monstrous plague of human locusts devouring and fouling the planet—more predatory than piranha fish and more suicidal than lemmings. Civilization "works," temporarily, for the privileged individual, but in the not-so-long run it could so easily be a speeding up of consumption that dissolves all life on the planet.

There is no question or possibility of abandoning technology and retreating into simple and sentimental anarchy. What we really need is a technology managed by people who no longer experience "self" as something foreign to the body and its physical environment. For it is precisely this interior conflict between ego and organism that underlies organized warfare and violent revolution, most especially when such violence is rationalized as being in the cause of justice and human betterment. No wars have been more ruthless and ravaging than "just" wars, fought in "defense" of religion, honor or principle. If war must be, give me rather a war to capture an enemy's wealth and territory, based on honest greed, in which I shall be careful not to destroy what I want to possess. But as civilized wars are fought for principle, so the technological "conquest of nature" is in fact being waged for the purely abstract satisfaction of making money, as distinct from the material and sensuous enjoyment of good food, beautiful women and elegant surroundings. Our greatest money-makers are largely puritans and nose-to-the-grindstone people who have neither taste nor time for material pleasures. We need a technology aimed, not at abstract and inedible dollars, but at caviar and excellent wines the whole world round.

Only a supernaturalist would deliberately press the button to set off nuclear warfare in the belief that his spiritual values are more important than material existence. And this involves the open or tacit supposition that the spiritual dimension is immortal, and that in heaven or on some higher level of vibration unaffected by bodily death he will continue his existence, congratulating himself on his fidelity to principle and wagging the finger of reproof at the suprisedly immortal souls of dialectical materialists, eating crow in the sky instead of pie. This simply goes to show that belief in the superiority and final authority of the rational, intellectual, conceptual and symbolic domain as the ultimate reality may be inconsistent with the survival of mankind.

Unexpectedly, naturalism is more consistent with the mystical vision of the world than supernaturalism, as should be clear from the suspicion in which mystics have always been held by the official establishments of Judaism, Christianity and Islam. Supernaturalism splits the cosmos into the unequal duality of creator and creature, spirit and matter, ruler and subject, ego and organism, and many an atheist is in fact a supernaturalist insofar as he is trying to regulate the physical order of nature by the logical order of language or mathematics. But a naturalist cannot consistently subscribe to the belief that he himself is in any way separate from his whole physical organism. He cannot, therefore, consider himself driven or victimized by his own organic processes, for his emotions and appetites and, indeed, the entire functioning of his body are his own doing, however spontaneous and undeliberate.

Once this is admitted, a further and essentially mystical insight comes into view. If I am my organism, I am also my environment. From the ecological and biophysical standpoints every organism goes with its environment transactionally: the one implies the other as buying implies selling, and front implies back, and the positive pole implies the negative. Thus every living organism implies not only the conditions of the immediate solar system, but also the entire constellation of galaxies. If a human body could be transported to another universe, careful study by the local scientists would eventually reveal that it came from an environment that included sun, moon, planets, Milky Way and the nebulae in Andromeda. For as the fruit implies the tree, the human organism implies a cosmic energy-system that "peoples" in the same way as a plant flowers.

Basically, then, "self" is not only the body but the whole energy-system that embodies itself in all bodies. The conceptual ego does not control this system any more than it controls the heart, but whereas the ego is your idea of yourself the total energy-system of the universe is what you are. People who realize this could be trusted with technological power, for they would respect the external world, with all its subtle ecological balances, as they respect their own bodies. They would work with it and not against it, as a sailor works with the wind even when moving in a contrary direction.

The basic point to be understood then, is that it is simply impossible to improve either oneself or the world by force. Because you yourself *are* both the organism and its environment, this is as futile as trying to lift yourself off the floor by your own bootstraps. Untold psychic and physical energy is wasted in this ludicrous enterprise, which, when seen to be absurd, is abandoned, releasing that energy for tasks that can indeed be accomplished. Trying to force a lock bends the key, for which reason a truly intelligent man never forces an issue. He resorts instead to *judo,* the "gentle way" of trimming one's sails to the wind, of rolling with the punch, and of splitting wood along the grain. Such intelligence is therefore the alternative to violence.

ALTERNATIVES

COUNTERACTANTS TO VIOLENCE
by Kenneth E. Appel

Kenneth Appel, former president of the American Psychiatric
Association, is Professor Emeritus of Psychiatry at the
University of Pennsylvania.

There are too many things that people are against—not enough things that people are for. They are against authority, war, traditional religion, ways of living, education, social institutions, family ways, traditional morality.

The needs of all the people must be met—many people's needs are not now being met. They need jobs to help eliminate poverty and hunger, they need training and education for work and the acquisition of skills for a technological economy, they need space for homes, recreation, chance for adventure and travel—and to relieve crowding. There is a positive correlation between crowding and size of families, health, the level of education, the ability to get job training, improved job status, mobility, the possibilities of change, ignorance and crime.

People need to feel they have a personal investment in business, industry and welfare, a stake in the community and an opportunity to make things different. Fulfillment of these needs helps to eliminate hopelessness, frustration and destructive aggression.

People are frustrated, aggressive and violent when a sufficient number of their primary needs are not met. In addition to the above, there are needs for a sense of personal worth. These are attained:

(1) through the use of abilities and achievement;

(2) through respect and appreciation from others, friendship from some, and love from a few—that is, through respect and appreciation from the community;

(3) through hope for personal growth or enhancement; and

(4) through belief in the possibility or probability of opportunities for the realization of the above.

"I am somebody because I can do things and because there are people who care." If these needs are not met, and there is a serious degree of frustration, then hostility, aggressiveness and the probability of violence result.

Work and confidence in the future create credit and security. Activity, do-ability, clearing of slums, new buildings for health, education and recreation give confidence and hope. New concepts of cities can be built by new partnerships of government and business.

Many vigorous efforts by discontented young people throughout the world illustrate involvement and desire for constructive change. The effort and vitality, even in blundering and irritating attempts, can be recognized as a dynamic for new starting points and endeavors.

Mitchell Ginsberg suggests the use of welfare funds to subsidize employment opportunities in public services, such as aides in hospitals, health and welfare services, schools, museums, libraries and sanitation services.

Encouraging evidence of the recognition of shared responsibility in the tragic acts of violence not long past is shown by a recent letter to a newspaper:

> *I don't understand why President Johnson, Rep. Boggs and other Americans high and low are insisting that "200 million Americans did not shoot Robert Kennedy." Of course we shot him. We all had a hand in it.*
>
> *Every time we let our children watch detective and spy shows on television where human life is constantly being killed in more and more original ways, every time we applaud movies like "Bonnie and Clyde" and allow our teenagers to see them, every time we hand our little boys guns and rifles to play with, every time we helped pull that trigger.*
>
> *Every time we did not teach our children to respect the rights of others, every time we let them have their way ("They're only young once"—"Boys will be boys") and looked the other way while our teenagers vandalized; every time we blamed the teacher for being mean*

to Johnnie and told Johnnie not to pay attention to that dumb old teacher; every time we ourselves lied and cheated our friends or customers or strangers, or the government—we shot Robert Kennedy.

Every time we allowed, and even taught, self-indulgence, instead of self-discipline; every time we said "Look out for Number 1," every time we insisted everyone must think like we do or they're no good—we killed yet another Kennedy.

No indeed, we are all responsible, and I don't know if I'll ever get over my share of the deed.

This indicates and suggests what parents, relatives, neighbors, friends, teachers, each of us, can do today—not in some distant time when conditions are better and people are more sophisticated.

Here are burdens belonging in part to all of us.

Here are things—something everybody can do—now.

Our children surely need firm discipline, but with the attitudes of love and support for the child himself. If authority is inconsistent or hostile and down-grading to the child, the result may well be hatred of parents and of society, and violence can be the end result.

As to war, much more is needed than proposals of negative action. Cessation of hostilities should be combined with positive proposals for rebuilding, for medical help and sanitation, education and economic help in terms of natural developments of a country's own culture. This could be done as a joint effort in the areas of economics, education, science and government, with contributions from the old with the developing countries. No nation would lose face in such an undertaking, and it would be a challenge to the resources, ingenuity, technology, social and administrative know-how of the countries in collaboration. It would not wipe out religious and ideological differences, but hopefully would use these to the advantage of all in a sort of ecumenism. This would involve both domestic and international relationships and organizations imaginatively in a new level of world cooperation.

TOWARD WORLD COMMUNITY NOW
by Harold D. Lasswell

Harold Lasswell is Ford Foundation Professor of Law and the Social Sciences at Yale University and author of *National Security and Individual Freedom*.

From the viewpoint of any competent observer of world affairs it is evident that the world community is a fundamental fact of life, despite the confusion and conflict that disturbs the evolution of a public order strong enough to maintain basic security and to foster the optimum realization of the promise of mankind.

The challenging and often puzzling question is why the elites of the world community continue to find it beyond them to substitute the politics of reciprocal threat by the politics of common interest. It would appear to be elementary wisdom to turn the billions of dollars now devoted to military purposes to the task of bringing into existence a globe whose inhabitants are well fed, well housed, well educated and well motivated to play responsible roles in life.

What's wrong?

It is important to understand how deeply the institution of war is integrated with the other institutions of man. Obvious characteristics of the arena of world politics are division and militancy; both depend more on the *expectation* than the love of violence. The significance of expectation is emphasized when we ask why the presidents and the prime ministers of the major powers do not meet in a summit conference, a confrontation that they promptly turn into a constitutional convention where they redesign the legal and governmental institutions of the world community. Why do they not accept the idea of a common police force in which national contingents are scrambled? Why do they not agree to the possibility of being voted down by the majority on issues that affect access to the means of production and enjoyment?

The basic answer to these queries is simple. The top elites are afraid to act boldly to introduce an inclusive system of public order on a global scale. Given their matter of fact expectations about the political

118

process at home and abroad, they are fearful of losing their power (if not their lives). Rival leaders, factions and parties stand ready to withdraw support from any president or prime minister, whether he is operating in a socialist or a liberal nation-state, who seems to be "selling out" to a foreign power, hence betraying his trust by compromising national security. Political leaders see no advantage in political suicide.

But what of the communications revolution that has annihilated distance in the transmission of messages? Or the travel revolution that can pick up a passenger in New York or Moscow, carry him around the world and deposit him in New York or Moscow in less than a day? Why haven't these technological wonders brought about a corresponding transformation of the minds and hearts of men?

The answers to these questions are not necessarily complicated. They give prominence once more to the role of expectations in the political map of the world on which decision-makers act. World elites are fearful of losing mid-elite and rank and file support if they allow foreign elite and rank and file support to obtain ready access to their publics. Hence the universalizing potential of the new technology has been controlled for parochial purposes. The divisions of the world political arena precondition the zones in which messages and people are free to circulate.

As a result mankind continues to live in psychoculturally segregated neighborhoods, a patchwork of ethnic and linguistic ghettos. The "brown" people are segregated in East and South Asia; the "black" population is mostly in Africa; the "white" people are in West Europe and the Americas.

It is true that expanded travel and communication have widened the experience of millions of men, women and children. It is no less true that the effect has been to widen the sense of identity *somewhat;* but the "somewhat" is short of all mankind.

What is the "identity" process and how is it affected? Each of us has a distinctive subjective experience: I am "I." But the boundaries of the ego ("I," "me") are vague; typically they include symbols of reference to other egoes as part of the "self" (parents, siblings, tribesmen, etc.). Some identifying symbols distinguish *our* self from the self of others ("Americans" versus "Chinese," and so on).

The significance of identifying symbols is that they are part of a more complex system whose function is to provide a map of expectation and a prescriptive code of behavior. The map is the perceived world of nations, parties, races, religions and the like; it includes images of how they look, what they want, how they feel, what they know and how they act. The prescriptive code is a set of norms for the self and others. It includes the demand to look after the needs and aspirations of family, tribe and nation. Some demands are directed to others, asking them to behave in various ways. So far as distant individuals and peoples are concerned the identifying images, demands and expectations may be very vague indeed. Given this thinness of perspective the individual member of the world community continues to be dependent on a stream of communication that is proliferated and polluted in conformity with the fragmented structure of the world arena and the apprehensive manipulations of the world elite.

In the light of the integration of the institution of war with the structure of every sector of the world community, we must conclude that the problem of moving toward an inclusive civic order in which violence ceases to play a major role is far from simple. It would appear to call for the cultivation of perspectives that are very different from traditional perspectives. *The institution of war,* for instance, is *part of a self-sustaining international system that survives by generating expectations on the part of influential people that they, the influential ones, will be relatively better off by continuing the system than by taking the risks involved in changing it.*

Can the violence system be changed into a nonviolent system? Can this transformation be brought about nonviolently? The answer, I submit, is yes. Without attempting at this moment to estimate probabilities, we can at least be explicit about the conditions that must be met. Evidently the fundamental inference to be drawn from failures to date is that structural changes depend on the timing of well-placed motivations for change. Elite members who initiate and support nonviolent change must be rewarded with power, respect and other value indulgences, rather than penalized by value deprivations.

The strategists of nonviolent change must therefore cultivate programs that emphasize simultaneity on a global scale, and that concentrate on those individuals and groups who are most likely to influence others. The obvious targets are the intellectuals (scientists, scholars, students) whether they are in academic, official or private roles. Whether we like it or not the educated and the semi-educated exert a relatively overwhelming impact on their fellowmen, chiefly because they have the greatest influence on the content of the stream of communication that mobilizes collective action in accepted grooves, or initiates new departures. The new departures may be mediated directly by the dissemination of the new, or indirectly by operating differentially on those who change the routines of fighting, producing or performing other institutional functions.

In this day of rapid, though partially controlled, communication and travel, all initiatives for structural change are likely to have worldwide repercussions and to do so at an increasing rate. The management problem is to expedite these repercussions and hence to strengthen the impact on decision-makers of the assurances of support that they receive for initiating nonviolent change. It must be made apparent to leaders and potential leaders, old or young, socialist or liberal, that they have more to gain by intensifying the discovery of common interest than by playing a separated and parochial game in world affairs.

Identities widen when experience broadens; and the communication experience is itself a precursor of quickened involvement. A relevant communications experience can be intensified by a collaborative experience, that is, by acting in concert. Common action ranges from joint discussion to joint demonstration; and to the harmonizing of both official and unofficial initiatives.

The traditional structure of the world community has emphasized the territorial divisions associated with nation-states and empires, city-states and tribes. As the modern pattern of science and technology moves toward universality, transnational pluralistic groupings multiply and provide gradations and linkages for collective action on a worldwide nonviolent scale. If we think of *public order* as sustained by potentially violent sanctions, our task is to strengthen world *civic order,* which relies on nonviolent sanctions in support of concerted action.

As a means of strengthening civic order on a global scale the promising strategy is to offer a wide range of *participatory experiences in initiating and perfecting policy structures and functions that typically fall outside the grooves of conventional public order.* The most relevant territorial zone to the modern world is not the nation-state but the great urban nuclei and their sustaining areas. Hence a major objective of programs of world civic order must be the cultivation of the metro-global community, meaning a world organized as voluntarily as possible among the emerging metropolitan centers of the globe. It is equally relevant to the evolution of a comprehensive civic order to hasten the growth of cooperative entities that in principle disregard territorial lines. This objective is the cultivation of a pluralistic community on a worldwide scale.

It is not beyond the wit of man to reorganize the global community along metropolitan and pluralistic lines. If the deliberate cultivating of such a world civic order is to gain momentum, it would be expedient for a single instrument to become the recognized channel through which the vast number of essential initiatives is able to achieve whatever degree of coordination is helpful. For this purpose a World Community Association would be appropriate, welcoming into its federated structure every territorial and pluralistic association of similar aim. The WCA would devote itself to the realization of the program implied by the slogan "Build World Community Now" or "Participate in Nonviolent Civic Order Now."

A territorial component of the WCA would be chapters in the metropolitan regions of the globe. It would be sensible to allow each individual member to belong to as many metropolitan chapters as he wishes. His dues could be adjusted according to the principles that might be applied in apportioning tax burdens in a reorganized world. The obligation could be defined according to the location of the individual's home, office, factory or farm; readjustments could be in accord with appropriate rules and procedures. Prior to obtaining control over official machinery at local and more general levels, the WCA would necessarily depend for income on membership fees and gifts and on the proceeds of collective enterprises.

In most countries it is feasible for the WCA to build world community now and to cultivate a nonviolent civic order by supplying services and opportunities for its members. Such a program is aimed at the preparation of a new world within the framework of the old.

The WCA can supply many voluntary services to its members. By arranging for group insurance WCA can provide income protection for individuals and obtain the capital required to provide supplementary medical, educational, recreational, housing and employment facilities. The members of the WCA who travel abroad and who welcome visitors from other countries can spread general participation in the growth of nonviolent civic order. Members can send their children, or encourage the sending of children, to educational institutions whose authorities and teachers are in tune with the objectives of WCA.

The WCA can widen the opportunities open to members by the development of economic enterprises. In some instances the Association will presumably launch business enterprises of its own. The WCA will be eligible to receive by a gift or bequest stock in corporate undertakings. In some cases cooperative forms of control can be used (e.g., majority stock control remaining in the hands of the Association, while minority control is given to consumers on the principle of one-share one-vote). The WCA may engage in mixed governmental and private enterprise.

Not the least promising potentiality is a network of WCA laboratories for research and development where scientists can work directly for mankind; and a network of civic observatories, where social scientists and other scholars can consider the social consequences and implications of global trends, including those in science and technology. Closely connected with these data gathering and processing operations would be the initiation of plans at all metropolitan, intermetropolitan and submetropolitan levels. Properly conceived, these plans would attempt to provide an environment, social and natural, in which children can develop personalities equipped with perspectives and proficiencies fitting them for citizenship in a world community devoted in practice, as well as in theory, to the dignity of man.

If movements toward a universal nonviolent civic order are to succeed they must be guided by shared comprehension of at least a few fundamental tools of thought. One is the distinction between value goals and achievements and specific institutions. In a divided world a principal factor in the perpetuation of division is the exaggerated importance assigned to particular ways of doing things in various national cultures and regions.

The articulate value goals of mankind are remarkably uniform. In recent years they have been enunciated in the Universal Declaration of Human Rights and in countless speeches and public documents. It is not difficult to grasp the point that a world community adapted to the dignity of man provides opportunities for widespread rather than narrow participation in *power,* as in voting; in *enlightenment,* as in access to a dependable flow of information and scientific knowledge; in *wealth,* as in enjoyment of the benefits of technologies of production; in *well being,* as in safety, health and comfort; in *skill,* as in opportunity for the discovery and training of talent; in *affection,* as in opportunity for free choice of friends and marriage partners; in *respect,* as in recognition of fundamental humanity and of individual achievement; and in *rectitude,* as in opportunity for achieving a responsible relationship to life through religious and philosophic orientation.

The institutions of mankind are unendingly varied, and if they are not to stand in the path of man's evolution, they must be subject to continuous appraisal. The criteria are their successes or failures in the shaping and sharing of values.

A helpful intellectual tool in the appraisal of institutions is the contextual principle.

According to this principle the effect of a doctrine or a technique depends on its relation to the community context of which it is a part.

Specific institutions do not automatically or invariably carry specific value consequences with them. Different results may be obtained by doctrines or techniques that appear at first to be incompatible.

It is an exemplification of the contextual principle that a moral doctrine gives different results when applied by true believers and by hypocrites. It is also compatible with the principle when a technique of production, such as the use of machinery, raises the standard of living in some countries but not in others—where, for instance, energy goes into the manufacture of weapons.

The members of the WCA can assist one another in identifying tendencies to assert exaggerated claims concerning specific institutional devices. While we can be certain of our commitment to human dignity, a nonviolent order is possible only if an experimental, exploratory, creative attitude is adopted in the consideration of ways and means. Institutional practices are collective guesses about net value advantages; what was effective in yesterday's setting may not be in today's.

In every part of the globe organized initiatives have been springing up on behalf of programs that are explicitly compatible with the strategy outlined here. Whatever can be done to bring these associations and individuals into more direct awareness of one another can contribute to a synchronization of motive and policy favorable to a world system of nonviolent civic order.

A major steppingstone in the path toward a world community of nonviolence is the perfecting of instruments for the monopolization of coercion in the hands of an inclusive system of public order. Such a monopoly is, in fact, an indispensable requirement of even a minimum level of world law and order.

However, inclusive monopoly of violence is extremely dangerous to human freedom unless it is itself a transition, and is perpetually challenged as a transition, toward a world order that is sufficiently well accepted to dispense with coercive violence. A system of world public order can be trusted to fulfill the overriding objectives of human dignity if and only if the world civic order is vigorous enough to achieve and sustain a network of institutions that remove provocations to violence and strengthen voluntary action to bring into being a comprehensive culture of freedom and responsibility.

The broad conclusion is that it is feasible to move toward a world community now; and that it is practicable to enlarge the scale of participation in nonviolent civic order now.

THE ESSENCE OF SECURITY

Pp. 145-158 of "The Essence of Security" from "The Essence of Security" by Robert S. McNamara, Copyright © 1968 by Robert S. McNamara. Reprinted by permission of Harper & Row, Publishers, Incorporated.

by Robert S. McNamara

Robert McNamara, former Secretary of Defense and president of Ford Motor Company, is now president of the World Bank.

... The planet is becoming a more dangerous place to live on, not merely because of a potential nuclear holocaust, but also because of the large number of *de facto* conflicts and because the trend of such conflicts is growing rather than diminishing. At the beginning of 1958, there were 23 prolonged insurgencies going on around the world. As of February 1, 1966, there were 40. Further, the total number of outbreaks of violence has increased each year: in 1958, there were 34; in 1965, there were 58.

What is most significant of all is that there is a direct and constant relationship between the incidence of violence and the economic status of the countries afflicted. The World Bank divides nations on the basis of per capita income into four categories: rich, middle-income, poor, and very poor. The rich nations are those with a per capita income of $750 per year or more. The current U.S. level is more than $2900, and there are 27 of these rich nations. They possess 75 per cent of the world's wealth, though roughly only 25 per cent of the world's population. Since 1958 only one of these 27 nations has suffered a major internal upheaval on its own territory.

But observe what happens at the other end of the economic scale. Among the 38 very poor nations—those with a per capita income of under $100 a year—no less than 32 have suffered significant conflicts. Indeed, they have suffered an average of two major outbreaks of violence per country in the eight-year period. That is a great deal of conflict, and, what is worse, it has been predominantly conflict of a prolonged nature.

The trend holds predictably constant in the case of the two other categories, the poor and middle-income nations. Since 1958, 87 per cent of the very poor nations, 69 per cent of the poor nations, and 48 per cent of the middle-income nations have suffered serious violence. There can be no question but that there is a relationship between violence and economic backwardness, and the trend of such violence is up, not down.

Perhaps it would be somewhat reassuring if the gap between the rich nations and the poor nations were closing and if economic backwardness were significantly receding. But it is not. The economic gap is widening. By the year 1970, over one half of the world's population will live in the independent nations which encircle the southern half of the planet. But this hungering half of the human race will by then command only one-sixth of the world's total of goods and services. By the year 1975, the dependent children of these nations alone, children under 15 years of age, will equal the total population of the developed nations to the north.

Even in our own abundant societies, we have reason enough to worry over the tensions that coil and tighten among underprivileged young people, and finally flail out in delinquency and crime. What are we to expect from a whole hemisphere of youth where mounting frustrations are likely to fester into eruptions of violence and extremism? Annual per capita income in roughly half of the 80 underdeveloped nations that are members of the World Bank is rising by a paltry one per cent a year or less. By the end of the century these nations, at their present rates of growth, will reach a per capita income of barely

$170 a year. By the same criteria the United States will have attained a per capita income of $4,500.

The conclusion to all of this is inescapable. Given the certain connection between economic stagnation and the incidence of violence, the years that lie ahead for the nations in the southern half of the globe look ominous. . . .

Violence anywhere in a taut world transmits sharp signals through the complex ganglia of international relations; and the security of the United States is related to the security and stability of nations half a globe away. But neither conscience nor sanity itself suggests that the United States is, should or could be the Global Gendarme. Quite the contrary, experience confirms what human nature suggests: that in most instances of internal violence, the local people themselves are best able to deal directly with the situation within the framework of their own traditions. The United States has no mandate from on high to police the world, and no inclination to do so. There have been classic cases in which our deliberate non-action was the wisest action of all. Where our help is not sought, it is seldom prudent to volunteer.

Certainly we have no charter to rescue floundering regimes which have brought violence on themselves by deliberately refusing to meet the legitimate expectations of their citizenry. Further, throughout the next decade advancing technology will reduce the requirement for bases and staging rights at particular locations abroad, and the whole pattern of forward deployment will gradually change. Though all these *caveats* are clear enough, the irreducible fact remains that our security is related directly to the security of the newly developing world, and our role must be precisely this: to help provide security to those developing nations which genuinely need and request our help, and which demonstrably are willing and able to help themselves. The rub is that we do not always grasp the meaning of the word security in this context.

In a modernizing society security means development. Security is not military hardware, though it may include it; security is not military force, though it may involve it; security is not traditional military activity, though it may encompass it. Security is development, and without development there can be no security. A developing nation that does not, in fact, develop simply cannot remain secure, for the intractable reason that its own citizenry cannot shed its human nature.

If security implies anything, it implies a minimal measure of order and stability. Without internal development of at least a minimal degree, order and stability are impossible. They are impossible because human nature cannot be frustrated indefinitely. It reacts because it must; that is what we do not always understand and what governments of modernizing nations do not always understand.

But by emphasizing that security arises from development I do not deny that an underdeveloped nation can be subverted from within, or be the victim of aggression from without or be the victim of a combination of the two. This can happen, and to prevent any or all of these conditions a nation does require appropriate military capabilities to deal with the specific problem.

The specific military problem, however, is only a narrow facet of the broader security problem. Military force can help provide law and order, but only to the degree that a basis for law and order already exists in the developing society, a basic willingness on the part of the people to cooperate. Law and order is the shield behind which development, the central fact of security, can be achieved.

We are not playing a semantic game with these words; the trouble is that we have been lost in a semantic jungle for too long and have come to identify security with exclusively military phenomena and most particularly with military hardware. It just isn't so, and we need to accommodate ourselves to the facts of the matter if we want to see security survive and grow in the southern half of the globe.

Development means economic, social and political progress. It means a reasonable standard of living, and reasonable in this context requires continual redefinition; what is reasonable in an earlier stage of development will become unreasonable in a later stage. As development progresses, security progresses, and when the people of a nation have organized their own human and natural resources to provide themselves with what they need and expect out of life, and have learned to compromise peacefully among competing demands in the larger national interest, then their resistance to disorder and violence will enormously increase. Conversely, the tragic need of desperate men to resort to force to achieve the inner imperatives of human decency will diminish.

I have mentioned that the role of the United States is to help provide security to these modernizing nations, providing they need and request our help and are clearly willing and able to help themselves. But what should our help be? Clearly it should be help toward development. In the military sphere, that involves two broad categories of assistance. We must help the developing nation with such training and equipment as are necessary to maintain the protective shield behind which development can go forward. The dimensions of that shield must vary from country to country. What is essential, though, is that it should be a shield and not a capacity for external aggression.

The second and perhaps less understood category of military assistance in a modernizing nation is training in civic action, another one of those semantic puzzles. Too few Americans, and too few officials in developing nations, really comprehend what military civic action means. Essentially, it means using indigenous military forces for nontraditional military projects, projects that are useful to the local population in fields such as education, public works, health, sanitation and agriculture—indeed, anything connected with economic or social progress.

It has had some impressive results. In a recent four-year period around the world U.S.-assisted civic action programs constructed or repaired more than 10,000 miles of roads, built over 1,000 schools and hundreds of hospitals and clinics, and provided medical and dental care to approximately four million people. What is important is that all this was done by indigenous men in uniform, and, quite apart from the projects themselves the program powerfully alters the negative image of the military man as the oppressive preserver of the stagnant *status quo*.

Assistance in the purely military sense, though, is far from enough. Economic assistance is essential. . . . Only the developing nations themselves can take the fundamental measures that make outside assistance meaningful. These measures are often unpalatable and frequently call for political courage and decisiveness. But to fail to undertake painful but essential reform inevitably leads to far more painful revolutionary violence. Our economic assistance is designed to offer a reasonable alternative to that violence. It is designed to help substitute peaceful progress for tragic internal conflict.

The United States intends to be compassionate and generous in this effort, but it is not an effort it can carry exclusively by itself. Thus it must look to those nations which have reached the point of self-sustaining prosperity to increase their contribution to the development and thus to the security of the modernizing world.

This brings me to the second set of relationships that I mentioned at the outset: it is the policy of the United States to encourage and achieve a more effective partnership with those nations which can and should share international peace-keeping responsibilities. America has devoted a higher proportion of its Gross National Product to its military establishment than any other major free world nation and this was true even before our increased expenditures in Southeast Asia. Over the last few years we have had as many men in uniform as all the nations of Western Europe combined though they have a population half again greater than our own.

The American people are not going to shirk their obligations in any part of the world, but they clearly cannot be expected to bear a disproportionate share of the common burden indefinitely. If, for example, other nations genuinely believe, as they say they do, that it is in the common interest to deter the expansion of Red China's economic and political control beyond its national boundaries, then they must take a more active role in guarding the defense perimeter.

Let me be perfectly clear. This is not to question the policy of neutralism or non-alignment of any particular nation. Rather it is to emphasize that the independence of such nations can in the end be fully safeguarded only by collective agreements among themselves and their neighbors. The day is coming when no single nation, however powerful, can undertake by itself to keep the peace outside its own borders. Regional and international organizations for peace-keeping purposes are as yet rudimentary, but they must grow in experience and be strengthened by deliberate and practical cooperative action. . . . The Organization of American States in the Dominican Republic, the more than thirty nations contributing troops or supplies to assist the Government of South Vietnam, indeed even the parallel efforts of the United States and the Soviet Union in the Pakistan-India conflict— these efforts together with those of the U.N. are the first attempts to substitute multi-national for unilateral policing of violence. They point to the peace-keeping patterns of the future. We must not merely applaud the idea; we must dedicate talent, resources and hard practical thinking to its implementation.

In Western Europe, an area whose burgeoning economic vitality stands as a monument to the wisdom of the Marshall Plan, the problems of security are neither static nor wholly new. Fundamental changes are under way, though certain inescapable realities remain.

The conventional forces of NATO, for example, still require a nuclear backstop far beyond the capability of any Western European nation to supply, and the United States, as I pointed out earlier, is fully committed to provide that major nuclear deterrent. The European members of the Alliance, however, have a natural desire to participate more actively in nuclear planning. A central task of the Alliance, therefore, is to work out the relationships and institutions through which shared nuclear planning can be effective. A practical and promising start has been made in the Special Committee of NATO Defense Ministers. Common planning and consultation are essential aspects of any sensible substitute to the unworkable and dangerous alternative of independent national nuclear forces within the Alliance. . . .

We now come to the third and last set of relationships the United States must deal with, those with nations who might be tempted to take up arms against us. These relationships call for realism, but realism is not a hardened, inflexible, unimaginative attitude. The realistic mind is restlessly creative, free of naive delusions, but full of practical alternatives.

There *are* practical alternatives to our current relationships with both the Soviet Union and Communist China. A vast ideological chasm separates us from them and, to a degree, separates them from one another. There is nothing to be gained from our seeking an ideological rapprochement. But breaching the isolation of great nations like Red China, even when that isolation is largely of their own making, reduces the danger of potentially catastrophic misunderstandings and increases the incentive on both sides to resolve disputes by reason rather than by force.

There exist many ways in which we can build bridges toward nations who would cut themselves off from meaningful contact with us. We can do so with properly balanced trade relations, diplomatic contacts, and in some cases even by exchanges of military observers. We have to know, though, where it is we want to place this bridge, what sort of traffic we want to travel over it, and on what mutual foundations the structure can be designed. There are no one-cliff bridges; if you are going to span a chasm, you have to rest the structure on both cliffs.

Cliffs, generally speaking, are rather hazardous places. Some people are afraid even to look over the edge. But in a thermonuclear world we cannot afford political acrophobia. President Johnson put the matter squarely: by building bridges to those who make themselves our adversaries "we can help gradually to create a community of interest, a community of trust and a community of effort."

With respect to a community of effort, let me suggest a concrete proposal for our own present young generation in the United States. It is a committed and dedicated generation; it has proven that by its enormously impressive performance in the Peace Corps overseas and by its willingness to volunteer for a final assault on such poverty and lack of opportunity that still remain in our own country.

As matters stand, our present Selective Service System draws on only a minority of eligible young men. That is an inequity, and it seems to me that we could move toward remedying that inequity by asking every young person in the United States to give two years of service to his country, whether in one of the military services, in the Peace Corps or in some other volunteer developmental work at home or abroad. We could encourage other countries to do the same, and we could work out exchange programs much as the Peace Corps is already planning to do.

While this is not an altogether new suggestion, it has been criticized as inappropriate while we are engaged in a shooting war. I believe precisely the opposite to be the case; it is more appropriate now than ever, for it would underscore what our whole purpose is in Vietnam, and indeed anywhere in the world where coercion or injustice or lack of decent opportunity holds sway. It would make meaningful the central concept of security, a world of decency and development where every man can feel that his personal horizon is rimmed with hope.

Mutual interest, mutual trust, mutual effort—these are the goals. Can we achieve these goals with the Soviet Union and with Red China? Can they achieve them with one another? The answer to these questions lies in the answer to an even more fundamental question: Who is man? Is he a rational animal? If he is, then the goals can ultimately be achieved; if he is not, then there is little point in making the effort.

All the evidence of history suggests that man is indeed a rational animal, but with a near infinite capacity for folly. His history seems largely a halting but persistent effort to raise his reason above his animality. He draws blueprints for Utopia, but never quite gets it built. In the end he plugs away obstinately with the only building material really ever at hand: his own part-comic, part-tragic, part-cussed, part-glorious nature. I, for one, would not count a global free society out. Coercion, after all, merely captures man. Freedom captivates him.

POSITIVE PEACE—THE PRESENCE OF JUSTICE
by Paul Martin

Paul Martin, statesman and diplomat, is Leader
of the Government in the Senate of Canada and Minister
without Portfolio.

No consideration of the problem of violence would be complete without reference to the part that it has played at the level of international affairs.

War, as Winston Churchill once remarked, is the story of the human race. So much of the experience of history seeks to suggest that it is in the nature of man to settle his differences with his neighbor by going to war with him. Naked force has been at the foundation of power since the dawn of history, and the philosophy of the power-seeker has been aptly summarized by Mao Tse-tung in the words: "Political power grows out of the barrel of a gun."

Attempts to ensure the prevention of war and to promote the peaceful settlement of disputes through international organization are a comparatively recent development on the international scene. One would like to believe that these initiatives indicate a growing refinement in the nature of mankind. Perhaps they do, but it is difficult to avoid the conclusion that they have been inspired as much by fear of the consequences of war as by moral revulsion against it. The technological revolution of our time has made the success of such endeavors a matter of urgent necessity. For the first time in his recorded history, man faces the possibility of extinction by weapons of mass destruction that he has himself created. The alternatives to violence on which the world has been relying since the end of World War II have had their roots in this stark fear.

The first attempt at substituting negotiation for war in the settlement of disputes as an international principle took place within living memory. The first International Peace Conference was held at The Hague in July 1899 at which a Convention on the Peaceful Adjustment of International Differences was drawn up. The first article stated in part:

"With a view to obviating, as far as possible, recourse to force in the relations between states, the signatory powers agree to use their best efforts to secure the pacific settlement of international differences."

When this convention was drafted, the world was about to enter the century of total war and mass destruction. Perhaps the statesmen who negotiated it at the turn of the century had some premonition of the shape of things to come. Be that as it may, their efforts were not successful, and two World Wars later we are still seeking the permanent formula for the avoidance of war that has so far eluded us.

We can, however, take heart from the fact that similar efforts have been consistently pursued since the first International Peace Conference took place. A second such conference was held in 1907 reiterating the principles established at the first. In April 1919, following the carnage of World War I, the Covenant of the League of Nations was adopted, the preamble of which stated that it was the aim of the contracting parties "to promote international peace and security by the acceptance of obligations not to resort to war." Some nine years later the United States and France took an initiative that led to the Briand-Kellogg Pact, condemning and renouncing war as an instrument of national policy.

Unfortunately the peacemakers were not prepared for the monstrous phenomenon of Hitler, and in their desperate determination to spare the world the horrors of a further war they allowed themselves to be intimidated by the bluff and bluster of this tyrant to the point where it became impossible to avert catastrophe. It took yet another World War and the advent of the nuclear age to strengthen the international community in its unity of purpose. The Charter of the United Nations, drawn up in 1945, laid even greater stress on the need to prevent international violence. The opening sentence speaks of the determination of the United Nations to save succeeding generations from the scourge of war that had brought untold sorrow on mankind. Article 33 of Chapter VI, which deals with the Pacific Settlement of Disputes, goes on to state: "The parties to any dispute, the continuance of which is likely to endanger the maintenance of international peace and security, shall, first of all, seek a solution by negotiation, enquiry, mediation, conciliation, arbitration, judicial settlement, resort to regional agencies or arrangements, or other peaceful means of their own choice."

Since the end of World War II it can be said that the international community has succeeded, through the incentive of fear, in preserving the fragile fabric of world peace, at least to the extent of preventing the outbreak of global or nuclear war. This success, however, has been due as much to restraint on the part of the great powers as to the efforts of the United Nations Organization itself. On more than one occasion the world has found itself poised dangerously on the brink, but from these occasions certain international guidelines have emerged. In its ruthless suppression of the Hungarian Revolution in 1956, the Soviet Union made it clear to the world that it was prepared to defend its sphere of influence in Eastern Europe by any means necessary. During the Cuban missile crisis in 1963, the U.S. made it equally clear that when its security was directly threatened it would go to any lengths in order to protect it. These two trials of strength and nerve served to establish a measure of international equilibrium and a tacit understanding between the two great powers of East and West, both confrontations being classic exercises in the technique of "thus far and no farther."

The United Nations played no effective role in either the Hungarian or the Cuban crises, although in other areas it has been active and not altogether unsuccessful. The first important test of the organization's capacity for collective action came in June 1950, with the outbreak of hostilities in Korea. It took three years to bring the fighting to an end, the efforts of the United Nations being greatly handicapped by the absence of Communist China from its counsels. No formula has yet been found to control the explosive situation in the Middle East, which has continued in a condition of ferment ever since the establishment of the state of Israel in 1948, although some of the Organization's most determined and constructive efforts have been concentrated in this area of unrest. The tragic war in Vietnam, to which no end is yet in sight, is the most grievous problem with which the world is currently confronted, and probably the United Nations' most serious area of failure to date. Nevertheless the United Nations Organization has achieved limited successes in its peacekeeping operations in various parts of the world.

The most satisfying progress that has been made so far in international relationships is in the control of nuclear weapons. A treaty signed in 1959 made the Antarctic continent a demilitarized zone. In 1963, the partial test ban treaty was concluded prohibiting nuclear explosions in outer space, under water or in the atmosphere. In 1967 a further treaty barred the use of nuclear weapons in outer space, and in the same year the states of Latin America and the Caribbean took steps to create a nuclear-free zone in their area. The most important breakthrough came on July 1, 1968, with the signing by the United States, the United Kingdom and the Soviet Union of a treaty to prevent the proliferation of nuclear weapons, a treaty to which 40 other nations are expected to adhere. A further encouraging development since the signing of the treaty has been the response of the Soviet Union to an American proposal for discussions aimed at achieving partial nuclear disarmament and a slowing down in the development of strategic nuclear delivery systems and anti-ballistic missile defensive systems.

These agreements are to be applauded, but they should be viewed with guarded optimism. They do not of themselves settle the basic political and ideological disputes that continue to threaten the peace of the world. It must be borne in mind that the non-proliferation treaty was opposed by certain states and that China in particular, itself a nuclear power, has denounced the treaty as a U.S.-Soviet plot aimed at establishing a nuclear monopoly. The treaty is open to criticism in that it denies to the smaller powers rights that it allows to the nuclear powers, and it is certainly vital to the treaty's success that the latter should recognize their obligation to protect the security of the non-nuclear powers.

Fear of extinction, fear of the unknown and terrible consequences of nuclear war, has thus made possible the advances in international relations which have so far taken place. Fear, however, is not an alternative to violence on which the world will be able to rely indefinitely. A prolonged period of peace can of itself give rise to dangers. In a world in which nobody has ever experienced the horrors of war, the deterrent effect of fear could well be tempered by the equally natural human emotions of curiosity as to what war is really like, and the age-old desire for expansion and aggrandizement. The only long-term alternative to violence must lie in the ennoblement of man's nature. We can hope that our continuing efforts to promote international understanding and to eliminate mistrust between nations will tend to elevate man's moral sense to a level consistent with that of his technological achievement.

International cooperation is an obvious and essential alternative to violence, but there must be an effective basis for cooperation, and this calls for more than a mere forum of discussion. It is a paradox of our age that in spite of the momentous technological developments we have witnessed in this century, we have yet to solve the age-old problems of poverty and ignorance. We are a very long way from perfecting our own environment even though we have succeeded in breaking through its confines. At a time when our technological skill has brought us to the threshold of a landing on the moon, millions of human beings continue to live and die in misery, the victims of mankind's most ancient scourges. It is little inspiration to the millions who continue to exist in a stone-age environment that the advance guard of humanity is poised to penetrate the vastnesses of outer space. In spite of man's achievements the have-nots of the world still greatly outnumber the haves. Such a situation is potentially explosive and the narrowing of the gap between the privileged and the underprivileged must, therefore, be regarded as one of the imperative alternatives to violence. Pope Paul VI stated in his fifth encyclical that "the new name for Peace is Development." This theme was enlarged upon by the Prime Minister of Canada, Pierre Trudeau, when addressing a convocation of the University of Alberta on May 13, 1968. He said, among other things:

Never before in history has the disparity between the rich and the poor, the comfortable and the starving, been so extreme; never before have mass communications so vividly informed the sufferers of the extent of their misery; never before have the privileged societies possessed weapons so powerful that their employment in the defence of privilege would destroy the haves and the have-nots indiscriminately. We are faced with an overwhelming challenge. In meeting it, the world must be our constituency.

If the underprivileged peoples of the world are to take their place in the sun, the fortunate nations will probably be called upon to accept greater economic sacrifices than have yet been fully envisaged. Yet they are sacrifices that pale into insignificance when the alternatives are considered. International peace cannot be maintained while gross inequalities abound and war calls for sacrifices of a far more grievous and far less constructive nature, the tragic war in Vietnam bearing ample testimony to this truth. The privileged nations have everything to gain by promoting the development of those less fortunate, and they must realize that something more than token aid is required. New concepts of international aid must be grasped if its effectiveness is to be guaranteed, and we should cease to think of aid only in terms' of handouts. For example, it is of vital importance to the developing countries that their trading prospects should be improved, and if a meaningful improvement is to take place the wealthier nations may need to revise their own trading patterns. A way must be found to enable the developing countries to find the markets that they so desperately need and without which they cannot progress. Unselfishness, or rather an enlightened self-interest that recognizes that the key to preserving the security of the fortunate lies in guaranteeing the security of the less fortunate, would seem to offer considerable promise as an effective alternative to violence.

In the pursuit of lasting peace the nations of the world face internal as well as external challenges. The eruption of discontent among young people is a recent development of particular significance. The widespread questioning of authority among the young is a reflection of the instability and turbulence of the world as a whole. It would be wrong to oversimplify this phenomenon, but the protest of the younger generation is basically a revolt against conformity with an order of society that they feel they had no hand in shaping. Violence is the most effective form of protest because it never fails to focus public attention upon grievances. The methods of protest are familiar, but the grievances are new. Those who are protesting are in general the articulate youth, those who are better educated and materially more fortunate than any previous generation. Their protest is not based upon the material deprivation that inspired the great revolutions of history, but on frustration brought about by nonparticipation in the institutions that govern their lives. The stimulus to protest is a feeling of helplessness induced by living in an insecure world.

It is interesting to note that studies that have been made in relation to Viet Cong successes in the rural areas of South Vietnam suggest that the revolutionaries tend to attract support among people who are politically rather than economically deprived. Pursuing this theme in a recent article in *Foreign Affairs*, Samuel P. Huntington concluded as follows:

> *Any suggestion for greater decentralization of authority in Vietnam is always met with the charge that it will encourage "warlordism," to which a strong Central Government is the only antidote. In actuality, however, as the earlier history of China, Vietnam and even Western Europe amply demonstrates, warlordism is the product not of efforts to provide a structured decentralized authority, but rather of efforts to maintain a narrowly based, centralized authority where it is inappropriate to the situation. Warlordism is the illegal, disruptive and violent way in which a centralized system is adapted*

to the realities of dispersed power. Warlordism is the alternative to the formal decentralization of authority, not a product of it.

In the recent past, the French, Bao Dai, Diem, each in different ways, attempted to perpetuate centralized authority, and in every case they weakened it. To strengthen political authority, it is instead necessary to decentralize it, to extend the scope of the political system and to incorporate more effectively into it the large number of groups which have become politically organized and politically conscious in recent years. Such a system might be labeled federal, confederal, pluralistic, decentralized—but, whatever the label, it would reflect the varied sources of political power. In the recognition of and acceptance of that diversity lies the hope for political stability in Vietnam.

If this argument is valid for South Vietnam, it is almost certain to have a wider application. The answer to the challenge of the young—their alternative to violence—could lie in the widening of opportunities for participation in the shaping of society. This implies an extension of representation, not merely in the organs of central and local government, but at every major institutional level—the schools and universities, the trade unions and professional associations, the corporations, the political parties, the churches. For these institutions, together with the organs of government, constitute the Establishment, and are therefore the levers of power and the instruments of change. Unfortunately, those who control them sometimes become bored, and resistant to change, and the institutions tend to stagnate as a result. From time to time they need reinvigoration, and there is no better formula for the stimulation of this process than an infusion of new blood. The methods of extending the range of individual participation would vary with the institution concerned and would need to be carefully considered, but the overall aim would be to widen the influences that can be brought to bear on decision-making processes wherever they take place.

In any just society, the right of protest must, of course, be protected. Perhaps the greatest internal challenge any nation can be called upon to face is that which arises from racial diversity within a population. The fact that friction so often develops where communities of differing origin come into close contact illuminates one of human nature's most tragic defects. Historically, the principal sufferers from these frictions have been the colored peoples of the world. For centuries they have been the victims of racial discrimination, with all that this implies in political, social and economic terms. The revolt against such discrimination, which was bound to take place one day, has in recent years erupted with an explosive suddenness. People of color throughout the world have become politically articulate, and it is as though a slumbering giant has come to life. New leaders have emerged to give expression to long-suppressed resentment and indignation; the colored peoples have found their voice and their capacity to organize.

Violence has been an inevitable concomitant of the struggle against racial injustice, but certain great humanitarian leaders have shown that there are effective alternatives to violence. The example of Mahatma Gandhi, who employed the technique of passive protest to great effect during the struggle for the independence of India, has been an inspiration to other leaders blessed with his great compassion. The outstanding advocate of nonviolence in the struggle against racial injustice was the late Dr. Martin Luther King, who was to the Negroes of America what Gandhi was to the people of India. As an alternative to violence, nonviolence sounds rather like a statement of the obvious, but it connotes something more than its face value would imply. It is in fact quite a militant alternative to violence, involving as it does civil disobedience, mass demonstrations, public obstruction and any means of protest *short* of violence.

In one of his last public pronouncements, Dr. King said: "We need an alternative to riots and to timid supplications. Nonviolence is our most potent weapon." These words clearly indicate that nonviolence is something more than passive submission. Dr. King, while urging restraint upon his people, sounded a call to action. In so doing he aroused many of the white people of America, as well as the Negroes, in the painful search for justice. He was fortified in his mission by his profound faith in the basic goodness of man and the great potential of American democracy. His leadership, his appeal to moral law, his spirit of moderation and his scrupulous concern about the means in pursuit of the end kept the process of gaining justice for the Negro on the road to a breakthrough. To his influence can be attributed the passage by Congress, in 1965, of the legislation that eliminated literacy tests for voters, provided federal registrars to assure the ballot to unregistered Negroes and marked the growth of the Negro as a political force in the South.

The fate of Dr. King is a grim reminder to us that the pursuit of alternatives to violence continues to demand its martyrs. Is it possible to keep faith when such men as he, and men such as Gandhi, John Kennedy and Robert Kennedy fall victims to assassins' bullets? The answer must be "yes." The revulsion that sweeps through the world when outrages such as these occur reinforces the good causes of mankind and weakens the power of those who would impede the march of progress and justice. The martyrdom of good men redeems the causes for which they fought, just as Christ, through his death, redeemed mankind. Martin Luther King demonstrated that it is possible to secure the redress of grievances without resort to violence. But he also warned men of good will against preferring "a negative peace, which is the absence of tension, to a positive peace, which is the presence of justice." We must recognize that timid conservatism has never succeeded in leading the world out of the shadows. Only a bold and experimental attitude can chart the course into the broad, sunlit uplands and guide the world toward the solutions it is seeking—the elimination of injustice, the reconciling of differences and the achievement of enduring peace.

TOWARD A WORLD OF PEACE UNDER LAW

"Conflict Resolution and World Education," adapted from Stuart Mudd, Ed.,
Dr. W. Junk, Publishers, The Hague, 1966, and Indiana University Press,
Bloomington, Indiana, 1967.

by Stuart Mudd

Stuart Mudd, former president of the International
Association of Microbiological Societies, is Professor Emeritus
of Microbiology at the University of Pennsylvania.

World law is, indeed, a necessary condition for world peace; but is it also a sufficient condition?

With improving communication and awareness have come rising expectations. Disease, undernutrition and malnutrition, lack of housing, lack of education, lack of hope for better conditions of life, are no longer accepted passively as the inevitable lot of mankind. In consequence we see political instability, coups d'état, civil strife, little wars and the looming horror of major wars. We see the emergence of sovereign states, too small and too poorly provided with resources and with leadership to be economically and politically viable, too competitive to be willing to associate themselves into groupings that can be viable. We see the population in particular of the developing countries increasing at rates out of all proportion to the feasible rates of development of human and material resources, with the result that already miserable standards of living deteriorate even further.

Cardinal Suenens of Belgium, in commenting on the magnificent encyclical *Pacem in Terris,* has written: "No man of good will can accept the fact that two-thirds of the world—two million of every three million men—do not attain the level of normal human development that technology places at the disposition of privileged peoples. This disproportion, this disequilibrium, hangs with all its weight on the peace of the world."

There is profound need that there be widespread understanding and passionate feeling that the unit of survival has become the human *species*, all of mankind. It no longer suffices that the goal of great religions should be individual enlightenment and release from the suffering of this world. It no longer suffices to seek individual, corporate or national wealth and power for the fortunate at the expense of the less fortunate.

To remake a world that is capable of peace under law will require all the love and compassion, all the vision and leadership, all the knowledge, skills and resources of which modern science, technology and art are capable. No less a goal than the good of all mankind will serve.

A world capable of permanent peace will need to have been modified in at least the five following categories:

(1) Development of human resources through education, technological training and public health measures.

(2) Development of material resources of agriculture, energy sources, forests, minerals, river basins and the riches of the seas.

(3) Control of population growth to realistic proportion in relation to available resources.

(4) Economic, political and legal association of states so as to become viable units.

(5) The development of skills in interpersonal communication and understanding, of mutual good will and of capacity for compromise and conflict resolution. The development of leadership with the vision and the will to achieve a world peaceful under law.

Of course it is possible to conceive of a world unified and pacified by despotic force, a sort of *pax terrestris*, under some hypothetical tyranny. It is hardly necessary to emphasize that this would not be a desirable world.

The intuition of Omar Khayyám, written centuries ago, has present relevance:

> *Ah, love! could you and I with Him conspire*
> *To grasp this sorry Scheme of Things entire,*
> *Would not we shatter it to bits—and then*
> *Remold it nearer to the Heart's Desire!*

The word in this quatrain to which I would direct attention is "entire," for the human state is now determined by a nexus of economic, demographic and political factors so complex as to negate the value of any *partial* solution of its problems.

It is, indeed, dangerously misleading to suppose that the ingenuity of science and technology can lift the burden of poverty and hunger in disregard of the demographic facts of life. The very same applications of public health measures that have been and are so dramatically increasing life expectancy in the developing areas of the world, in the absence of corresponding measures to control fertility, have precipitated the tragic disproportion between population growth and the development of resources. This disproportion is increasing the gap between the more fortunate and privileged parts of the world and the less fortunate. This disproportion unquestionably increases the misery of a large segment of mankind, is a basic factor in economic and political instability and is a menace to the peace of the world.

Happily a wave of understanding of the necessity for controlling population increase is now absorbing the thoughtful and responsible leaders of the world. Great institutions of government, of education and of philanthropy are concentrating on questions of motivation and of the operational realities of fertility control. The Economic and Social Council of the United Nations on July 29, 1965, took an epochal step by voting to "request the Secretary-General to provide advisory services and training in action programs in the field of population at the request of governments."

It is encouraging to note that governments as well as responsible individuals, both in the more and the less affluent parts of the world, are aware of the necessity, if a better quality of life for their citizens is to be achieved, of bringing their population growth into proportion with their resources. It was further noted, by Dr. Emily Mudd at the Conference of the International Union of Family Organizations held in Vienna in July 1968, that the ideal of family size held by young people throughout Western Europe and the United States is increasingly approaching two to three children per family, and that this optimum is indicated as realistic by the trend of current statistics.

Technical advances within the last few years, specifically the anovulatory pill and intra-uterine contraceptive devices, have changed the whole prospect for the better. There is now hope that the age-old proportionality between fertility and mortality can be re-established through reduction of fertility rather than through increase of mortality.

To gain time for this demographic revolution in the developing areas of the world, development of human and material resources must be energetically pursued. The subject is too vast to be discussed at this time except in the most general terms. It may be stressed, however, that introduction of modern methods of agriculture, discovery and efficient utilization of new sources of energy and of mineral wealth, multipurpose development of the great river basins for flood control, irrigation and hydroelectric power, involve operations that far transcend national political boundaries. A relevant example is the Mekong River Basin Development, in which many nations are participating, and which, if the area could be pacified, would contribute enormous resources to the political units of the area.

The fragmentation of empires into small sovereign states, the civil strife within those states, may represent necessary stages in the evolution of human self-determination and freedom. However, if these states are to become economically and politically viable, counter-trends must somehow be established toward cooperation and association into mutually supportive regional groupings. Tribal and national rivalries must become subordinated to common interests.

There are vital tasks peculiarly appropriate to a world university such as planned by the World Academy of Art and Science. Leaders must be trained for many lands and many special undertakings; such men and women should be dedicated to the welfare of mankind; they should also be trained to high competency in one or more essential operational areas: professional, technological or political, as the case may be. Researches should be undertaken with regard to the manifold necessities of a world changing at an unprecedented rate.

Abba Eban, Foreign Minister of Israel, has referred to the tendency of those with great political power to become preoccupied with small issues, and the opportunity of those with small political power to concern themselves with great issues. Surely not the least of the challenges in today's world is the evolution and refinement of the image of a world in which people can live together in good will and mutual cooperation, at peace under world law.

THE ROLE OF SCIENCE—SOME CAUSES AND CURES
by Glenn T. Seaborg

Glenn Seaborg, former chancellor of the University of
California at Berkeley, is the chairman of the
U.S. Atomic Energy Commission.

I would like to discuss two general aspects of alternatives to violence. First, our ability to eliminate violent acts stemming from human desperation based on physical want; and secondly, our ability to reorient human thinking away from violence—eliminating "the climate of violence," to use the current expression.

Being a scientist, I will look at this subject mainly from the standpoint of using the tools of our scientific age—logic and reason, and energy and technology—to help us overcome our problems.

I believe that a major step to eliminating much of the violence our world suffers today is to eliminate as much human deprivation as possible. I know there are many who will disagree with me that deprivation is a major cause of violence today, who might point out how many human beings have always suffered in silence—without resorting to acts of violence—how many go to bed hungry each night without having committed armed robbery or murder, how many suffer the indignities allied with poverty without openly rebelling by acts of vandalism, looting or arson. But times are rapidly changing—they have already changed. All the poor and the meek no longer believe they will inherit the earth. They only see their children inheriting their misery. Nor do even the religious among them believe their suffering will be rewarded in the kingdom of heaven. More people every day remind them of how many others enjoy the fruits of the earth. And in our crowded world with its modern communications to compound the interfaces of poverty and wealth, privileged and deprived, it is impossible for them not to be painfully aware of the growing disparities existing between themselves and others. In addition, these disparities build daily and so do the frustrations that go with them because of the pressures that our modern world exerts.

But unilaterally to condemn these pressures and the technological causes of the growing interfaces is a pointless exercise because these forces are also among the most constructive forces of our society, and they can be used to narrow many of the gaps and eliminate many of the frustrations that cause men to resort to violence. We must take the more positive approach of using as much of our knowledge, resources and power as we can to reduce the economic and human pressures that are at the root of much of today's violence. I believe that we must attack these root causes now, and with fullest use of every applicable technology, even though such a campaign may not show the immediate results that some might claim for many of the suppressive measures to eliminate violence.

We may speak of law and order as being essential to a progressive society, but the highest form of law and order is not that which is maintained by fear and repression. It is the self-imposed law and order created by a society in which every human being respects and values every other human being because their individual and common efforts generate a better life for all. This is the social compact that every person must recognize and support. If we are to survive in today's crowded, technologically centered world there must be a reorientation of human values and goals so that everyone realizes how his own greatest potential is reached within the framework of a totally progressing society. Then we must move beyond the concept that everyone is also his brother's keeper. We must build a civilization that dynamically balances the individual and social wills of peoples, communities and nations. But all this can take place only if we begin now with a greater effort to reduce as much as possible the misery that so many people still suffer due to unfulfilled basic needs.

To accomplish this we will have to undergo some changes in attitudes and outlook that have restricted our acting in the moral manner to which so many so frequently give only lip service. One of our difficulties lies in resolving the very basic conflict we have between fulfilling our own needs and those of the community. I mean this in an individual sense and in the larger terms of nations and the global community. Our natural instincts are at the root of this conflict as we all have the instinct of survival, the desire to provide for ourselves and our immediate families. Added to this has always been the almost self-evident knowledge that sharing diminishes our own existence and future. Try as we may, very few of us instinctively believe "it is better to give than to receive"—especially if we have ever suffered any form of insecurity or deprivation.

But today we have a greater chance to loosen these psychological shackles—to act more like the moral men we claim to be. I think we are on the verge of proving that there is a crossover point, where community intelligence and effort—with accumulative science and technology—can provide us with such an abundance that men everywhere can enjoy a new level of freedom from want. This is not in defiance of any economic or physical laws. Hard work and sacrifice, resources and time are still essential, but we can achieve a new degree of efficiency, of return on our investment. In a sense, this new abundance is a pay-off unfolding from the centuries of collective intelligence that will eventually show us that in our Scientific Revolution one man's gain no longer has to come out of the hide of his fellow man—as it did in our Industrial Revolution.

I believe that somehow science and technology, if properly developed and applied today, can change our rigid belief in those precepts that have at times made men act less than human. When we no longer have to view each other as competitors for survival perhaps in time we can actually change human nature—or at least those aspects of it that are no longer essential.

That time is rapidly coming, but today we are suffering a transitional period in which the much heralded promises of a better life have not yet been fulfilled for most people—where expectations race far ahead of real gain, and this accounts for most of the unrest and turmoil in the world.

I think that, properly applied, science and technology can reduce worldwide violence in another way—by reducing the basis of historically motivated tensions between peoples and nations. Many of these historical differences have an underlying physical cause that can be eliminated. Let me give a hypothetical example: Countries A and B have been "natural enemies" as long as they can remember. Their history books perpetuate myths about each other's evil, and they are sporadically at war with one another. But behind much of their "natural" enmity is the fact that both are short of water and have access to the sea through a single disputed area. As a result, they spend millions of dollars on arms to fight each other and propagandize against each other, keeping their part of the world under constant tension and dividing other nations in their support.

Now let us suppose that the "other nations," anxious to settle this secondhand dispute and reduce their involvement, propose a solution. Through an international organization they suggest means, based on new technological advances, that can solve at least some of the physical problems of countries A and B. One suggestion is the construction of a very large nuclear desalting plant to supply fresh water to an area that cannot get water from a river claimed by the other country. Another suggestion is the construction by nuclear excavation of a new port and a connecting canal for the country that needs better access to the sea.

Let us go one step further and say that these previously impossible but still expensive projects were financed through the international organization with money released by a negotiated reduction in arms on the part of both countries A and B.

When the projects were completed and in operation we might see the beginning of a new era for both countries, where competition could be shifted from an arms race to a challenge to see who could be the most productive with their new resources. Then new "bridges" might begin to be built between the two nations—perhaps at first only the resumption of diplomatic ties, but then an exchange of some students and technicians. Eventually, a new feeling might develop between the two nations and, hopefully, a new generation in each country might eliminate in their children's textbooks the historical hatred that their forebears had perpetuated for centuries because these "natural enemies" always fought for land and water.

This, of course, is a hypothetical and perhaps oversimplified and overoptimistic example, but it has some basis in fact—enough, I hope, to make the point.

A similar point could be made in many other areas, materially, geographically and politically speaking. Through cooperation and the fullest exploitation of science and technology we can eliminate the exploitation of each other. Enough food can be grown for a reasonably controlled world population. Hunger does not have to be a reason for national or world tension. We have only begun to make proper use of the world's material resources and energy sources. International cooperation and rational, farsighted planning can advance developing nations and help to close many of the gaps in living standards around the world. The sacrifice on the part of the advanced nations to assist more vigorously in these efforts would still be minimal compared to the cost of perpetuating the arms races and the mistrust brought about by the tensions of an unbalanced humanity—unbalanced physically and psychologically. But to do all this we must be determined to put modern science and technology to its fullest, most constructive, most humane use.

Exploring briefly another aspect of alternatives to violence that science and technology might effect, let me touch on the so-called "climate of violence" idea that is so much in the limelight today.

Because of its tendency to focus on, analyze and amplify social problems, as well as technical ones, our culture has a tendency to aggravate and perpetuate many of its ills. Too many times our modern communications media generate heat where they should shed light. This is not because of any inherent evil in the system or the intentions of the men who guide it. There are a number of factors involved.

The first seems to be a natural proclivity on the part of human beings to highlight evils, wrongs or mishaps. I cannot comment on the psychological reason for this (perhaps other authors in this volume may touch on that) but the old dictum "No news is good news" seems to be true. We look for and seem to expect trouble. Daily hard-won gains, new improvements and signs of progress—except for the sensational "breakthrough" variety—we take for granted. A thousand lives routinely saved any one day will never make the headlines. A single act of violence will. A responsible citizen offering an important constructive idea or program will rarely be seen on the television news programs, but the demagogue advocating extremist action will usually get the benefit of a national audience. The story of the accomplishment of honest officials and employees is no story, but the misdeeds of one corrupt person invariably will be on page one.

If, added to this phenomenon, is the impact of the accumulation and focusing of these items in our mass media and the impact of today's media themselves—their sound, their pictures, their immediacy—there definitely is a social "climate" created that more often than not tends to be depressing and debilitating, that often seems to generate greater ills.

There is another factor that compounds this problem. It is that in their need for speed and wide coverage, the media tend to give an oversimplified view of our world and its problems. Too many half-truths, innuendos and opinions come across as hard facts—facts upon which public opinion is formed and democratic action based. As a result, rash judgments are too often formed and harsh, unwise action taken or necessary programs shouted down.

But how can our technological age correct this situation for which it seems to be so much at fault? Perhaps one way is by using our technology, and more of it, to increase and reinforce the flow of *positive* news and information. Responsible citizens—business and civic leaders, educators and government officials—must become better propagandists —in the good sense of the word—and capture a larger share of the public imagination. They must recognize the educational impact of the communications media, not as something apart from "formal education" but as a most important and relevant part of our total educational process. I am not talking about educational television and radio as most people think of it today. I am thinking in terms of infusing into the entire medium—by public pressure, by commercial incentives, by laws when necessary—a healthier, more purposeful outlook—one that will be inducive to a climate of constructive vitality rather than destructive violence.

In realizing the power of our communications media I recognize the dangerous potential of using its technologies for any degree of "thought control." But are our films, television and radio programs today any less thought-controlling or influential in their present state? And not to utilize these public educational tools in a more positive way to influence the course of society reduces our freedom by reducing our ability to understand and act rationally in this complex and rapidly changing world. In the final analysis we may well live up to the image of ourselves that our mass media portray. I think we can greatly improve that image.

In conclusion then, I believe that we can find alternatives to violence in many constructive uses of modern science and technology. We must put these forces to work to fulfill the promises they have already created. If we can use them to bring bread to men's bodies, knowledge to their minds and a new spirit to their hearts, we may achieve far more than end to violence—we may achieve the highest form of peace.

MANKIND'S MORAL MALADY
by Arnold Toynbee

Arnold Toynbee is a British historian and the
author of *A Study of History* and *Change and Habit:
The challenge of our time*.

The quest for alternatives to violence ought to be given the first place on mankind's crowded current agenda. This item should come first because it is the most urgent of all and is also the most difficult. It is urgent because, for man, violence has become suicidal now that the advance of science, applied to technology, has armed local sovereign states with atomic and bacteriological weapons. At the same time the elimination of violence from the conduct of human relations is not going to be easy. Human nature is potentially violent because life itself is. Every living organism is a miniature counter-universe. In organizing itself it has staked a claim to be a separate universe in itself. This claim commits an organism to attempting to set itself up as a center of the true universe, of which an organism is in truth no more than a part; and, in committing itself to exploiting the rest of the universe in its own self-centered interest, an organism is committing itself to the use of violence against other parts of the universe if there is a conflict of interests between one self-assertive organism and its competitors.

There are, of course, some social species of organisms. Man and the social insects are the two conspicuous examples of this type. To be a social organism is painful, for this is a biological reality that is a logical contradiction in terms, and consequently every specimen of any social species of living creature is in a perpetual state of tension between its two built-in instincts of egoism and altruism. Moreover, altruism can be an insidious mask for egoism magnified through being multiplied from the singular into the plural. Man is said to be the only known species of mammal in which specimens of the species fight each other to the death. The term "mammal" stands for maternal love, and human beings practise the un-mammalian activity of slaughtering each other because their sense of brotherhood with their fellow men as such is overruled by their sense of social obligation to the particular tribal fraction of mankind to which they belong. It is significant that the criminal institution of war—the use of impersonal, organized mass violence against fellow members of the same species—is not peculiar to man, though apparently war is waged by man alone among the mammals. War is also waged by ants, and ants are a social species whose social system is still more elaborate and more tyrannical than man's is.

Possibly ant communities can afford to go on waging wars with each other. The social insects' technology is impressive, but it is built-in, and it is therefore static. Man's distinctive psychic attributes of consciousness and a consequent power to choose are also built-in, but the products of this built-in human intelligence are not static. Its products that take the form of science applied to technology are progressive and cumulative. The progress of technology has been gradually gathering speed, and at the present day its rate of acceleration is portentous. Science and technology are morally neutral sources of power. They can be used at will for either good or evil. There is a terrifying disparity between present-day man's power and human morals. Man's average moral level is still the same as what it has always been. Self-centeredness (in theological terms, original sin) is born afresh in every newborn child. On the other hand, present-day man's power is immeasurably greater than his Palaeolithic predecessors' was. Today, human violence is not only the shocking moral evil that it always has been; it is now also a deadly danger to the survival of the human race. We have therefore to find alternatives to violence if we are to save ourselves from committing mass suicide.

One obvious expedient is to try to divert our innate proneness to violence from public and private criminal activities into more innocent and less dangerous channels. Institutionalized violence does not have to take the form of war. There are alternative institutions through which human pugnacity can discharge itself. One of these is sport. The rival supporters of competing teams can work off their aggressive

feelings with only occasional loss of life. The players themselves perform better morally than the spectators. The moral ideal of "sports-
manship" is a high one. It is the modern equivalent of medieval
chivalry. The sportsman's moral code requires him to be scrupulous in
abiding by the rules of the game, to contend without animosity while
contending with all his might, and to accept defeat without rancor.

Another obvious outlet for human violence is the conquest of further realms of nonhuman nature. During the first million years of
human history, man's pugnacity must have been wholly absorbed in
man's struggle for existence with other species of life on this planet. It
was only as recently as about thirty thousand years ago that man won
a definitive victory over all of his nonhuman opponents except microbes,
of which he was unaware, and sharks. Within the last hundred years
we have been discovering and defeating microbes, we have reached
this planet's North and South Poles, we have scaled its highest and
most precipitous mountains, and we have learned how to fly in its air-en-
velope. But we are still only at the beginning of conquering the deep
sea and outer space, and here are two vast fields in which man can
still find vent for his aggressiveness by pitting himself against nonhuman
nature.

Of these two still unconquered realms, the deep sea is both the near-
er and the more remunerative. Now that the world's human population
is exploding, while our consumption of nonself-reproductive raw ma-
terials is increasing prodigiously, we shall have to look more and more
to the waters of the sea for our food and to the sea's bottom for our minerals. Our planet's seas seem likely to yield its human conquerors a
more valuable return than can be expected from our moon's dust, but
spacemanship does have one advantage over deepseamanship. The
ocean has limits; outer space, so far as we know at present, may be infinite.

Sport and the conquest of new realms of inanimate nature are good alternatives, as far as they go, to fratricidal outlets for human violence.
But the opening-up of these channels is not going to be enough by itself. This is only a superficial remedy for mankind's dangerous moral

malady. Human beings will continue to vent their pugnacity in assaults upon each other unless and until the psychological and social causes of mutual animosity are diagnosed and eliminated. Today the whole world is seething with unrest, and this is boiling over all too frequently into violence that does not stop short of bloodshed. This worldwide unrest is manifesting itself in many forms, but, when we probe, we find everywhere one common underlying cause. Human beings are committing acts of violence because they feel that they are being treated not as persons but as things, serial numbers, ciphers; and, in too many cases, they have found by infuriating experience that recourse to violence is the only means by which they can extort attention to legitimate claims and genuine grievance.

Alternatives to violence will not eliminate violence unless we also succeed in removing the principal present cause of violence, and this cause is the effacement of human personality by the more and more impersonal organization of human affairs. We have to find ways of enabling people once again to participate personally in discussions and decisions that are of personal concern to them. This is going to be a hard problem to solve. Man has now become the slave of the technology with which he has equipped himself for liberating himself from his former servitude to Nature. He has discovered that he has merely exchanged one servitude for another, and the tyranny of his own man-made environment is proving more onerous than the tyranny of the natural environment that he has shaken off. Man's personality is now being dwarfed by the quantities, magnitudes, and speeds with which his triumphant technology has overwhelmed him.

The elimination of violence has become imperative, but we shall not succeed in persuading man to forbear from violence till we have released him from the bondage that is goading him into violence today.

𝕏

PRODUCTION STAFF FOR TIME INCORPORATED

John L. Hallenbeck (Vice President and Director of Production),

Robert E. Foy and Caroline Ferri

Text photocomposed under the direction of Albert J. Dunn and Arthur J. Dunn.